T0179438

Corporate Governance

Internal Audit and IT Audit
Series Editor: Dan Swanson, Dan Swanson and Associates, Ltd.,
Winnipeg, Manitoba, Canada.

The Internal Audit and IT Audit series publishes leading-edge books on critical subjects facing audit executives as well as internal and IT audit practitioners. Key topics include Audit Leadership, Cybersecurity, Strategic Risk Management, Auditing Various IT Activities and Processes, Audit Management, and Operational Auditing.

Project Management Capability Assessment: Performing ISO 33000-Based Capability Assessments of Project Management
Peter T. Davis, Barry D. Lewis

Auditor Essentials: 100 Concepts, Tips, Tools, and Techniques for Success
Hernan Murdock

How to build a Cyber-Resilient Organization
Dan Shoemaker, Anne Kohnke, Ken Sigler

Fraud Auditing Using CAATT: A Manual for Auditors and Forensic Accountants to Detect Organizational Fraud
Shaun Aghili

Managing IoT Systems for Institutions and Cities
Chuck Benson

The Audit Value Factor
Daniel Samson

Corporate Governance: A Pragmatic Guide for Auditors, Directors, Investors, and Accountants
Vasant Raval

Corporate Governance

A Pragmatic Guide for Auditors, Directors, Investors, and Accountants

Vasant Raval
Professor Emeritus
Creighton University

CRC Press
Taylor & Francis Group
Boca Raton London New York

CRC Press is an imprint of the
Taylor & Francis Group, an **informa** business
AN AUERBACH BOOK

First edition published 2020
by CRC Press
6000 Broken Sound Parkway NW, Suite 300, Boca Raton, FL 33487-2742

and by CRC Press
2 Park Square, Milton Park, Abingdon, Oxon, OX14 4RN

CRC Press is an imprint of Taylor & Francis Group, an Informa business

International Standard Book Number-13: 978-0-367-46886-6 (Hardback)
International Standard Book Number-13: 978-0-367-86275-6 (Paperback)

Library of Congress Cataloging-in-Publication Data

Names: Raval, Vasant H. (Vasant Harishanker), 1940- author.
Title: Corporate governance : a pragmatic guide for auditors, directors, investors, and accountants / Vasant Raval.
Description: Boca, Raton : CRC Press, 2020. | Series: Internal audit and it audit | Includes bibliographical references and index.
Identifiers: LCCN 2019056025 | ISBN 9780367468866 (hardback) | ISBN 9780367862756 (paperback) | ISBN 9781003031796 (ebook)
Subjects: LCSH: Corporate governance.
Classification: LCC HD2741 .R38 2020 | DDC 338.6–dc23
LC record available at https://lccn.loc.gov/2019056025

Visit the Taylor & Francis Web site at
www.taylorandfrancis.com

and the CRC Press Web site at
www.crcpress.com

Auerbach Publishing

To my soulmate
Prafulla

Contents

About the Author

Vasant Raval received his Doctor of Business Administration degree from Indiana University in 1976. Prior to joining Creighton University in 1981, he was a faculty member at the University of Windsor, Canada, for six years. After a long, productive tenure at Creighton University, he was awarded professor emeritus status in 2019. A graduate of University of Mumbai (B.Com.) and Indiana State University (MBA), he has also worked as a consultant, management accountant, and auditor in industry and government. His research and teaching interests include executive financial fraud, corporate governance, information ethics, information security, accounting education, and managerial accounting. Most of his research is applied in nature, and is qualitative and multi-disciplinary. He holds professional certifications in information systems audit and control and in management accounting. He is a member of the Information Systems Audit and Control Association (ISACA) and currently serves on the governing board of the Academy of Global Business Research and Practice (AGBRP).

An author/coauthor of over 70 papers and four books, Vasant served as Associate Dean and Director of Graduate Business Programs (1987–1996), and as Chair of the Department of Accounting (2002–2005) at Creighton University. Between 2002 and 2010, he was a board member and chair of the audit committee of two public companies in the USA, and also served on the audit committee of Douglas County, Nebraska, USA He enjoys reading, traveling, and water coloring.

Foreword

The corporate governance environment is fraught with tension and complexity. Tension emanates from inherent conflicts infused into the human condition. Even when we endeavor to pursue the wellbeing of others, self-interest is never far behind. Moreover, interest-based claims from an array of stakeholders – including shareholders, employees, governments, and communities – often present competing demands. When these relational complexities are layered upon pragmatic challenges of providing goods and services that meet the demands of a constantly changing marketplace, formidable challenges are presented.

The modern corporation has managed to navigate these challenges successfully, albeit with some mistakes and failures along the way. Governance practices have evolved to address the dynamics of changing sources of tension. Past failures often become catalysts for change, and human efforts to avoid repeating past mistakes often focus on laws and regulations – which helps to explain their expanding role in corporate life. At the governance level, laws and regulations are translated into policies and algorithms that drive compliance efforts, which are critical components for governance models.

Rules rooted in history can serve as guides, but they cannot foretell the needs of the future. Effective governance requires creative and strategic judgments for firms to thrive in a world of innovation and change. These strategies demand more flexible and consultative processes, which are capable of drawing from specialized knowledge and experience and adapting to dynamic conditions.

Dr. Raval brings a keen understanding of this tension and complexity to this book, which is designed to provide an accessible and helpful map to assess this environment. His efforts are informed not only by academic theory, but also by personal experience as an auditor and board member. He is a reliable guide because he has traveled this landscape before, and he knows it well.

Readers from different academic and professional backgrounds will find that his book provides lucid explanations of key concepts, institutions, and processes, as well as helpful schematics to illustrate relational complexities within systems that have emerged in the governance environment. Blending theory and pragmatic guidance, he also manages to highlight problems that continue to perplex and challenge us. Dr. Raval's guidance will empower governance professionals and those who advise them to meet those challenges in the years to come.

Edward A. Morse, Professor of Law and McGrath North
Mullin & Kratz Endowed Chair in Business Law,
Creighton University School of Law

Preface

It has been a long time since I first thought about writing a book on corporate governance. It is a field that is very old in its elemental form and yet is constantly evolving. Many disciplines have a stake in it, including economics, finance, accounting, law, leadership, management, and organizational behavior. An intriguing area, but at the same time, it is difficult to set its boundaries and view the whole picture.

A primary purpose of this book is to provide as complete a picture of the current state of corporate governance in the USA as I could. I find numerous resources that discuss specific aspects of corporate governance, but few show the entire picture and how different components dovetail with each other. To represent the whole, I start with foundations of governance, identify players in the area, discuss the triad between shareholder, the board, and management, and determine key issues in various aspects of corporate governance. For this, I had to draw essential threads from the theory, regulatory requirements, empirical research, media coverage, and my own personal experience. Each of these sources has its limits. For example, regulation often leans on the goal of compliance which is not enough to draw the complete picture. And empirical research is relatively new in this field and often is constrained by the number of variables controlled in the analysis, something one cannot fully achieve in practice. My own board experience was with two public companies, each with less than one billion dollars in annual revenue. Although not representative of the entire economy, it was enough to excite me to look into governance issues much more deeply. Besides, most challenges in corporate governance, I believe, arise at the early stages in the company's lifecycle, so the exposure proved to be relevant.

This book integrates and illustrates. A variety of different concepts are involved in governance, but how they relate to one's role in

I

Cornerstones

CHAPTER 1

Governance Matters

An overarching purpose of governance is to maintain trust in those who manage others' interests. The idea of governance applies to any group or entity, not just corporations. Take, for example, the neighborhood homeowners' association. It directs and controls what happens to the neighborhood in the immediate future and in the long run. The association initiates rules such as how the park inside the neighborhood will be used, where in the neighborhood speed bumps should be installed, and how pets will be handled in the public areas by their owners. In addition, the association enforces covenants that deal with the external look of each house, approves modifications to existing structures, and addresses complaints regarding violation of the covenant by any of the members. The governance structure permits the neighborhood to preserve its esthetics, help maintain the infrastructure such as roads and parks within the neighborhood, help protect the area from criminal activities, and keep the valuation of homes attractive. Many of these benefits would not occur if the houses in an area were not subject to governance by the homeowners' association. In essence, the association is trusted by the homeowners to do the right thing in their best interests. The cost of membership imposed on each owner is probably worth the discipline imposed on the neighborhood as a whole.

What works for a small organization becomes almost a necessity for a corporation with fiduciary accountability to its investors. At the core of corporate governance is a system that directs and controls the organization. Corporate governance is an evolving discipline that has been around for as long as public limited companies have existed. In recent years, corporate governance is clarified as GRC – governance, risk, and compliance – thus embedding the major governance responsibilities of risk management and compliance with the laws and regulations into its fold. As such, implicit in effective corporate governance is an interplay of several disciplines including accounting, finance, risk management, leadership, law, information technology, communication, and organizational behavior.

The purpose of corporate governance is to direct and control the activities of an organization by establishing structures, rules, and procedures for decision making. There is no set formula to translate this into what it means for a corporation; every case is different. Take, for example, a company that provided IT outsourcing services and due to continued growth, set up a major offshore center for this purpose. The idea was to benefit from access to skills at a very reasonable price. Practically, almost all client services were performed by this center with about ten thousand employees at the overseas center. The board considered the significance of the offshore center and attendant risks and decided that it would meet at the offshore location at least once every year for a longer than an average board meeting. As is evident in the board's decision, the business model, company's maturity stage, rate of growth, and changing risks should dictate appropriate governance steps. The governance in action is highly influenced by the complexity of the firm, uncertainty faced by the company, and the need for adaptation in changing environments.

MEANING OF GOVERNANCE

Governance means to regulate internally. The term *governor* in the field of engineering implies some mechanism that will measure and regulate the key outcomes of the device. An example is the centrifugal governor which regulates the machine's speed by exerting centrifugal force on rotating weights driven by the machine output shaft. Synonyms for governance include protector, steersman, and pilot. Each term describes some component of governance but, by itself, is not sufficient to express the overall spirit of governance. Collectively, these terms imply the need to govern – to protect, steer in a certain direction, or to pilot its trajectory and control its flight path. In engineering, the device is separately identifiable from the mechanism that regulates the performance of the device. In corporate governance, at least notionally, one may identify the company and its management as the "device" and the board of directors as the "mechanism." In the future, this idea of physical separation may be defied as, for example, in the case of a driverless car, where the car itself has the artificial intelligence to self-govern its particular journey.

As long as the owner and the business are essentially the same (that is, the owner directly controls the business), there is no need for a separate force to regulate the business. However, once the owner is separated from the management of the business, the owner – who now has very little control over the firm – becomes concerned about how well the business is doing. A corporation as a separate legal entity does just this; it separates the owners – providers of equity – from the management of company operations and strategy.

Corporations may be public companies or private companies. In private companies the owners are likely to be somewhat hands-on in the management of the business. As a result, there may not be as severe a need to govern as there would be for a company whose voting shares are publicly traded and owned by many, often numerous, investors. Foreign public companies that participate in the U.S. financial markets are, for all practical purposes, treated the same as public companies. The shares of foreign companies are usually listed in the U.S. financial markets as American Depository Receipts (ADRs), a negotiable certificate issued by a U.S. depository bank representing a specified number of shares, perhaps even a fraction of a share.

The separation of shareholders from management is accompanied by a vast amount of equity invested by the shareholders; their financial well-being is tied to how well their company is doing. After all, they are the ones who put at risk their investment in the owner equity of the company; although the management may be managing the company, they are at the risk of losing their investment if the company does not do well. At the same time, as a group, they wield considerable influence as providers of capital they invest in the company.

Shareholders and Management

If you look at who has invested in the voting shares of a company, you might find individual investors, banks and other financial institutions, retirement funds, charities, mutual funds, hedge funds, and exchange traded funds (ETFs). Such dispersed ownership may be appropriate for raising equity, but it certainly does not lend itself to owners having an intention or interest in direct management of the company. Today's complex businesses working in a dynamic environment require the expertise of dedicated professional management.

By design, shareholders agree to not get involved in the management of the company. And the managers agree to do the best they can to achieve the goals of the company directed primarily toward increasing shareholder equity in the business. So, the relationship is mutual: shareholders benefit when the company prospers, and management is rewarded as they lead the company to do well. What could go wrong in this relationship? Perhaps management fails to deliver or expends a disproportionate amount of resources to do so. It could be that management chooses alternatives that are more (or less) risky according to the owners, or that are not what the owners would pick. Thus, there is a built-in tension between the two.

An additional factor contributing to the complexity of the relationship between the shareholders and management is the issue of information asymmetry between the two. Management runs the show and, therefore, has all the data and information they need; on the other hand, the shareholders do not have access to information unless, and only to the extent, required by regulatory measures. While full access to all company data is neither desired nor expected by the shareholders, they do expect that information necessary for the governance of management will be available to them in a timely manner and in appropriate detail.

Finally, even with the arrangement of having professional management conduct the affairs of the company to grow value for the shareholders, the dispersed group is too large and practically unable to manage directly their agent, the top brass in the company. To solve this problem, shareholders elect a group of representatives as directors to form the board of directors. The board in turn provides oversight on management in the interest of the shareholders. Conceptually, another layer of principal-agent is added: management (agent) reports to the board (principal) who is an agent of the shareholders (principal). Thus, the burden of governing the company falls on the few organized as the

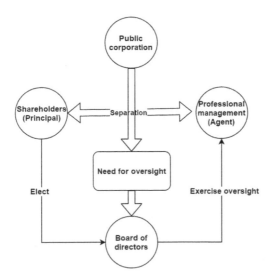

FIGURE 1.1   Agency in corporate governance.

board of directors of the company. Figure 1.1 provides an overview of the agency in corporate governance.

AGENCY PROBLEM

The idea of an owner having an agent manage the affairs of the owner-entity is not new; it has surfaced in various contexts. An apartment complex can hire a fulltime resident manager to manage the complex, a city can outsource the running of its mass transit system to another entity, and a shopping mall can hire services of a security firm to ensure that the mall is secure and people visiting or working in the mall shops are safe. The owner is called the principal and the manager, the agent. The principal-agent relationship is articulated in the widely known agency theory.

Within the context of the agency theory lies the agency problem or agency dilemma. Take, for example, a medical doctor's clinic that has acquired a new diagnostic machine. The machine is expensive, and the clinic would like to generate as much cash flow from it as possible in a relatively short period of time. The doctor may desire to recommend more of his patients for the diagnostics available through this machine, although in some cases there may be little need for the diagnosis. The patient trusts the doctor as his agent, but the outcome for the patient turns out to be more expensive and less fruitful!

The agency problem vividly illustrates that conflicts of interest may exist in an agency. Where conflict of interest emerges, the behavior of management – the agent – may not be aligned to the best interests of the shareholders – the principal. To manage their risk, owners would want to control senior management to generate management behavior congruent with shareholder interests. For this, the shareholders may deploy control mechanisms such as the following:

A. Regularly scheduled meetings between shareholders and management, for example, quarterly conference calls.

B. Publicly available media coverage of the company and the industry to which it belongs.

C. Pay-for-performance: an instrumentality designed in the compensation plans for the top executives wherein the shareholder interests are aligned with management incentives.

Agency Costs

Agency costs are a result of the possible deviation of agent behavior from the principal's expectations. Where such deviations are anticipated, the principal may develop measures to control such behavior; this, in turn, will result in agency costs. Unexpected deviations, while they cannot be controlled, will still result in some losses or other consequences, which are also a part of agency costs. The aggregate agency costs are normally classified as follows:

- Bonding costs: Costs of preplanned mechanisms agreed between the shareholders and management. These include proactive initiatives that will stabilize and align shareholder expectations with management's behavior. A performance-based compensation plan for top executives is an example of bonding costs.

- Monitoring costs: Costs incurred to observe and control management's behavior and to verify the results of the company financial performance through an independent audit. While excessive monitoring intrudes on management's freedom to steer the enterprise, too little monitoring could cause behavior contrary to shareholder expectations. As a result, moderation in monitoring activities is a desirable attribute.

• Residual loss: Residual losses arise from conflicts of interest which cannot be controlled due to lack of alignment between shareholder and management interests. Consequently, management misbehavior causes additional costs or losses to the shareholders.

Figure 1.2 provides an overview of the origin of agency costs.

Other Theories

While the agency theory has gained a great deal of attention in the corporate governance field, competing theories have been proposed. These include transaction cost theory, resource dependency theory, and stewardship theory.

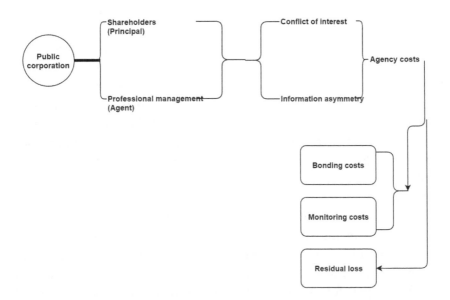

FIGURE 1.2   An overview of the agency costs.

Transaction Cost Theory (TCT) provides insights into why organizations are structured in certain ways and how they cope with uncertainty. If assets to be deployed by the firm are too specific (that is, have limited alternative uses in the outside market), chances are, the firm would prefer to own or control such assets. This reduces the amount of uncertainty. If the environmental uncertainty stems from the supply-side of inputs, it is likely that the firm would consider vertical integration of its operations by acquiring the sources of supply. For example, an oil refinery would also own crude oil producing facilities. The understanding of the organization structure, how it is staged to cope with uncertainty, and how it is changing over time in response to changing uncertainty is important from the perspective of risk management and resource allocation within the firm. Strategic decisions, such as make-or-buy, can be contextualized and assessed effectively using insights from the TCT.

An organization is essentially a collection of resources, tangible and intangible. The mix of resources owned or controlled by the organization results in the strength or power to the organization. This potentially powerful mix of assets is leveraged in dealing with the external factors, such as the customers, suppliers, and competitors. Management in this perspective is co-opted onto the common goal of shareholder value maximization. According to this theory, called the stewardship theory, the board members become key partners in helping management create alliances, exchanges, and strategic partnerships, thus reducing uncertainty and improving reliability of the company performance. In this context, board members provide valuable advice, create preferential access to information and resources, and establish legitimacy in relation to external entities. Multiple board memberships are valued in this context, for they allow relatively easy access to opportunities for the company.

Whereas the agency theory emphasizes conformance and compliance under the assumption that management may not act in consonance with the best interests of shareholders, the stewardship theory proposes that the goals of the board of directors (shareholders' representatives) are aligned with those of management and, therefore, a proactive and cooperative mode of governance is appropriate. Shared common agenda with full support for each other (board and the management) is implied in the stewardship theory.

In sum, no single theory paints a complete picture. The stewardship theory focuses on the alignment between the board and management, while the agency theory is centered on possible gaps, or misalignment in the objectives of the two – the board and management – and the consequent need for monitoring. The TCT uniquely stands out as the one that focuses on internal organizational structures and how these help manage uncertainty that the firm faces. Overall, it appears that the agency theory has gained considerable foothold in helping develop corporate governance perspectives; other theories have provided complementary perspectives missing in the agency theory, or are otherwise useful in developing a better understanding of the governance context.

Wherever the destiny of two entities (management and shareholders) is tied together, dependency occurs. While dependency cannot be avoided, the fact that their futures are intertwined cannot be ignored. As a result, a mutual bond between the two needs to be supported. A glue that binds the two is trust in each other. Without the trust, or in a violation of trust, less than desirable outcomes may occur, hurting either or both entities. In corporate governance, the concept of trust is central to support the separation of investors from the entity they invest in, represented primarily by management.

TRUST IN THE AGENT

The society runs on trust; it cannot function without people and organizations trusting each other. Predictability, efficiency, and reliability are some of the outcomes of trusting others. The city transit bus shows up on time, taking you to your desired destination. A Lyft driver picks you up for a ride to the airport and safely gets you to the airport in time for you to take the flight. Every household picks up and properly bags their waste for the city crew to collect it from the curb. These and numerous other duties we perform are the outcome of trusting people and organizations within society. The breakdown of trust would mean chaos, ruled by the rulebreakers commonly known as the hawks!

Trust – which is always given (or placed), not received – is fundamental to both trade and investments. Without trust in the economic system, the flow of resources into the economy will not occur. Investors need to be able to trust the financial system to put their savings to work

CHAPTER 2

Conceptual Foundations

Generally, a person is an entity distinctly responsible for his or her deeds. Centuries ago, the law broadened the definition of a legal entity to include corporations, that is, organizations that were incorporated and thus existed separate from their owners. In a society, individuals, groups, corporations, and other organizations build relationships that require trust of the party that looks after their interests. For example, two competing teams expect the referee to be objective and independent without any bias toward the outcome of the match. Similarly, a deaf person would expect that the translator responsible for conveying his message to his doctor protects his interests by truthfully converting the sign-language rendition into English.

An entity that, in a legal (or ethical) relationship with another, takes care of the other entity's money is called a fiduciary. The term fiduciary is derived from the Latin word *fiduciae*, a relationship of trust. The owner of a motel, for example, would trust the manager to take care of his interests in the motel. This would translate into various behaviors: ensure that all cash receipts are fully accounted for, that the motel premises are safe and protected, patrons are satisfied in terms of facility and services promised, etc. The manager is supposed to be competent in performing his duties and should be independent. A hallmark of independence is the absence of conflict of interest. As an example, a manager could create a conflict of interest by signing a contract for cleaning linens for the motel with a relative using better than market rates for such services. The manager is accountable to the owner for protecting the investment and for getting the best possible return on the

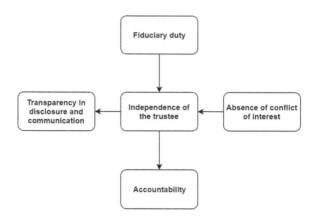

FIGURE 2.1 Fiduciary duty.

motel. It is also the duty of the manager to maintain a high level of transparency in disclosure and communication with the owner. To illustrate, masking critical information or cooking the books and presenting a biased financial picture would result in a violation of transparency. The nucleus of fiduciary duty is presented in Figure 2.1.

SHAREHOLDERS AS OWNERS

In corporate governance, a fiduciary relationship exists between shareholders and the management of the company they own. As a separate legal entity, the company still has a bond with its owners – the shareholders. Owners have the residual rights to their stake in the business and thus take on the risks of the business, although their liability is limited to what they invest in the company. The owners' bond with the company is essentially a bond with its management; often, the company and its management are referred to as synonyms, for the company is run by the management and for practical purposes, management is responsible for the company's acts.

Over the past centuries, the share of influence between the shareholders and management has shifted. The history of corporate governance has experienced three phases, beginning with what is called entrepreneurial, transitioning to managerial, and more recently to fiduciary governance. Early on it was the owner-entrepreneur who wielded more influence over the business, and management was essentially subordinate to the owner. This changed over time as the business environment became more complex and businesses grew larger where management expertise formed the core of business success. Top executives had a greater say on how the company was run while the owners became more passive. This era of managerial capitalism waned over time and the focus turned to fiduciary duties of management toward the company's owners. In this phase, it was clearly recognized that management has the duty to protect owner interests and operates as an agent of the owners. More recently, there has been an explicit recognition of interests of other stakeholders, such as employees, in addition to the affirmation of fiduciary duty toward the shareholders.

Those owning shares in a company change over time, and some existing owners may change their level of ownership, that is, the number of shares owned. At the launch of a company, investor subscription to shares goes directly to the company as owner equity in return for shares issued to the subscribers. Once the public offering of shares takes place, the shares are then traded in the financial market through a designated stock exchange, such as NYSE Euronext or NASDAQ. Resorting to the stock market, any investor can liquidate ownership of shares by selling them, in part or in full, and any investor can become a shareholder by buying shares of the company in the open market.

Shareholder or Stakeholder?

A great deal of debate surrounds the issue of whether corporate governance should take shareholder perspective or stakeholder perspective. Shareholder perspective suggests that the company exists to maximize returns to the shareholder in the long run, while the stakeholder view emphasizes that the company as a part of the economy has duties to all of its stakeholders, including customers, employees, and the community in which it is located. The former is labeled as an "ends" approach and the latter, a "means" approach. This is because the former focuses on the end goal, not explicitly considering how it is reached, and the latter stresses the ways in which all contributors to the value creation are recognized in the process of generating outcomes such as growth in employment and new jobs, innovation, positive social outcomes, and wealth creation.

Some argue that the shareholder perspective emphasizes greed and maximization of profit at any cost, thus suggesting that this is a narrow path in direct conflict with morality. This appears to be a fallacy. To serve the owners' interests should not necessarily be in direct conflict with ethical behavior. Whether one takes the "ends" approach or the "means" approach, the ethical conduct of business is not suggested as a compromise to be struck in the interest of the bottom line.

Whereas the debate surges on one or the other option, the reality is that both are an integral part of today's corporations. In the long run, a firm cannot optimize its value without regard to the wellbeing of all stakeholders. For example, if employees are unhappy at work, they would not be quite as productive or participating to their best in the innovation and growth of the firm. Even investors intuitively know this, as evident in the investor interest in funds that focus on social responsibility or ESG (environmental, social, and governance) concerns. As a result, it is important to think of both perspectives as central to a company's success, although the degree to which the two are integrated in a company may vary.

The recognition that all stakeholders are important to the long-term success of the company is clearly delineated in a 2019 Statement on the Purpose of a Corporation by Business Roundtable, an association of CEOs of America's leading companies, summarized in Table 2.1. However, given the history of successful large companies in America, it appears that this articulation is symbolic of current practice rather than a new commitment. While the broader stakeholder perspective is difficult to argue against, there are limits to its implementation. First, the company needs to be profitable and should have the necessary resources to go beyond some threshold of stakeholder recognition. Blake Mycoskie, a do-gooder, realized that he had to have resources to provide for the needy on a large scale. He therefore created TOMS, Shoes for Tomorrow, generated profits and donated a pair of shoes to needy children for every pair the company sold. Without resources, the desire to help stakeholders could remain unsatisfied. Second, while there is some clarity on how to measure shareholder value, the metric to measure benefit to stakeholders other than shareholders is lacking; more research and experimentation is necessary to determine satisfactory measures of stakeholder benefits. This may only be a short-term handicap and not a hurdle in the long run.

TABLE 2.1 A statement on the purpose of a corporation

Statement on the Purpose of a Corporation of the Business Roundtable, an association of CEOs of America's leading companies:

The member CEOs of many large and reputable corporations share a fundamental commitment to all their stakeholders:

- We will lead the way in meeting or exceeding **customer** expectations.

- We will compensate our **employees** fairly and provide important benefits, including supporting them through training and education that help develop new skills for a rapidly changing world. We foster diversity, inclusivity, dignity and respect.

- We will deal fairly and ethically with our **suppliers**, and serve as good partners to the other companies, large and small, that help us meet our mission.

- We support the **communities** in which we work. We respect the people in our communities and protect the environment by embracing sustainable practices across our businesses.

- We generate long-term value for **shareholders**, who provide capital for us to invest, grow and innovate. We are committed to transparency and effective engagement with shareholders.

Source: Adapted from www.businessroundtable.org.

It should be noted, however, that fair and ethical treatment of all stakeholders is important, and thus cuts across all stakeholders, not just suppliers. Also, fostering diversity, inclusivity, dignity, and respect is an objective worth considering for all stakeholders, not just employees. Transparency and effective engagement are important characteristics of all communications, regardless of the stakeholder.

While the amalgamation of shareholder and stakeholder interests is crucial in the destiny of a company, the law appears to focus mainly on the shareholder perspective. The law and regulations essentially are driven by the goal of shareholder protection and thus on the preservation and growth of capital markets where asset allocations take place. While no company does well without having good rapport with all stakeholders, ultimately, what matters is the view of how the company performed. This view currently is heavily weighted on data like share price performance and return on stockholders' equity. The research on triple-bottom line – social, environmental, and financial – has yet to produce acceptable overall metrics that measure company performance. But senior management motivation is tied to how their compensation is structured. Currently, all efforts seem to have been called upon to maximize shareholder value and, thereby, executive compensation.

Agency Theory

As discussed in Chapter 1, when the company is separated from owners, the interests of the owners are in the hands of those who manage the company. Some call this a contractual relationship, while others view it more broadly. Regardless, it is important for the owners, having yielded the managing function, to put in place mechanisms that hopefully will restrain management from (a) not doing a wrong thing (e.g., abuse of privileges for personal gain) and (b) not performing at best levels (e.g., becoming myopic). The owners are a principal and the management representing the company, the agent. The principal-agent relationship and issues and challenges involved in the relationship have been discussed extensively in the literature as the agency theory. Often, several mechanisms deployed in corporate governance can be traced to the agency theory.

The benefit of exercising control over management comes with costs of monitoring. These include the principal's monitoring costs, the agent's bonding costs, and residual loss. The principal's monitoring costs include outlays incurred in the supervision of management; a board member's compensation serves as an example. The agent's bonding costs include any costs of interaction with the shareholders; this would include any cost of communication with the shareholders. The residual loss points to any losses or deviation from expected performance that arises despite the attempts to control management. Management's decision to invest in a project with risks abnormally high compared to shareholder intentions to take risks is an example where a residual risk materializes if the project fails.

The agency theory identifies broadly the issue and challenges from the separation of ownership and management. However, it does not specify how this decoupling will be managed through oversight of management in the interests of the owners and, as well, for the economy and society. The theory shows why the challenges arise; however, it does not provide a functional architecture to generate solutions to the agency problem in today's complex corporate environment. For this we need to turn to corporate governance frameworks.

New expectations of corporate governance go far beyond addressing the so-called principal-agent conflict. In governance of the firm, contextual considerations lead to a more holistic framework. For example, the governance risk of a company depends on factors such as the complexity of the business model, how the company is structured, how it processes information and, generally, how it copes with uncertainty. When all of the factors relevant to GRC are considered, a holistic framework of corporate governance emerges.

CORPORATE GOVERNANCE FRAMEWORK

In corporate governance, as in many other cases, a one-size-fits-all approach does not work. Many variables are likely to impact governance in a particular company. The culture of the domicile country, life-cycle stage of the firm, industry to which it belongs, diversification and globalization of the company, and the applicable laws and regulations – these are some of the variables that would make up the overall picture of governance in the company. The nature and mix of governance measures and practices is likely to change over the life of the company, as it moves from initiation to contagion, to control, and finally to maturity stage. Presumably, the age of the company is one of the factors that determines the maturity of the governance process in the company. For example, the dynamics of governance at Uber, a ride-sharing company, are quite different from those at IBM, an information services giant.

This governance mosaic must have an overarching platform upon which the governance plan would rest. Without it, there would be no basis for a company to assess if its approach to governance is cohesive, integrated, and focused. Companies need a framework or a set of principles to build a robust governance program. Almost all professions rely on frameworks to design, validate, and operate a plan of action. For example, internal and external auditors may depend on the COSO (Committee of Sponsoring Organizations of the Treadway Commission) framework to execute or evaluate a system of internal controls, and if the presence of information technology in the organization is pervasive, they may trust the COBIT (Control Objectives for Information and

Related Technologies) framework to build trust in the system. One such framework in the corporate governance arena is the ACG, or Aspirational Corporate Governance framework.

Aspirational Corporate Governance

J. R. Galbraith, a profound researcher in organization design, put forth a proposition that greater uncertainty requires a greater amount of information processing between decision makers during the execution of the task in order to achieve a set level of performance. Because uncertainty limits the organization's ability to preplan, the organizations resort to various, usually complex, structures to increase their ability to preplan, to improve upon the flexibility to adapt to their inability to preplan, or to decrease the level of performance required for continued viability. More than 50 years since his publication, we realize how complex the corporate structures, processes, and practices have become to address today's complicated issues and challenges faced by companies.

Facebook, for example, has launched a new business segment in cryptocurrency. To accommodate its vastly different nature of business and high levels of uncertainty surrounding it, the company created a separate business entity called Calibra, led by experts in macroeconomics, monetary policies, electronic payment ecosystems, and information technology. This high uncertainty project requires the leadership of the company to recruit on its team of collaborators almost 100 established companies whose interests are tied to new developments in cryptocurrency. As a result, the company will have access to multiple organizations in a loosely networked form to address uncertainty as it unfolds. Calibra's separate identity within Facebook allows it to move fast and adapt quickly to changes unfolding over time. To facilitate this, the variety in the organization structure has to align with what the organization has set out to achieve while dealing with uncertainty.

For an organization to adapt, that is, to control its destiny, it must respond to changes in its environment. For this, organizations design, operate, and evaluate control mechanisms guided by a control framework. The control mechanism has to have the flexibility to respond to new out-of-control situations; otherwise, it would be ineffective in dealing with deviations from expectations. Resorting to the concept of requisite variety, organizations attempt to ensure that in the repertoire of controls there is at least one response to every out-of-control situation. The requisite variety in control mechanisms is complementary to the organization design. The alignment between the two ensures adaptability of the organization to its dynamically changing environment.

In proposing a corporate governance framework called Aspirational Corporate Governance (ACG), Turnbull identifies three parameters: requisite organization to address company complexity, requisite variety in control mechanisms to address uncertainty, and adaptive capacity to provide for self-adjustment.

- Requisite organization parameter warrants that capability of the organization must be matched with the company complexity.

- Requisite variety to address uncertainties implies that there is flexibility in the company's control mechanisms to respond to an out-of-control situation. In other words, there is at least one corrective step for every deviation from the expected behavior. A viable control system should be able to handle the variability of its environment.

- Adaptive capacity provides complementary means by which ACG systems can respond to empower stakeholders to reduce their uncertainty or to transfer risks away from stakeholders to make uncertainty acceptable.

For example, Facebook patrons were exposed to "deep fakes" or videos that have been digitally manipulated in misleading ways. Facebook recognizes its responsibility to protect online discourse on topics of interest to the society (e.g., elections), and to give users control over their data and experience on the Facebook platform. With proper policy changes and their implementation, the company can deliver appropriate governance objectives. Its vast resources ensure much more capacity to respond than smaller rivals like Twitter and Reddit. The company effectively adapts to moderating of content and protecting proper public discourse from rogue users.

The ACG framework provides a high-level understanding of corporate governance in action. The framework recognizes that uncertainty is a primary source of risk and risk mitigation begins with uncertainty.

The greater the uncertainty, the greater the likelihood that the affected organization has the appropriate complex structure to address the uncertainty dynamically. The example of third-party risk management (TPRM) illustrates this well. If your company has several thousand suppliers spread around the world and connected to your network, they become active connections to your company's networks and infrastructure and their risks are then inherited by your company to some degree. The assessment of third-party risks to your company and addressing those risks is a critical step in your company's governance. Because of differences in nature, types, and criticality of uncertainty faced by organizations, there exists a wide variety of organization structures and control mechanisms to adapt to uncertainty.

PRINCIPLES OR PRESCRIPTIONS?

While helpful, the ACG framework does not translate into precise prescriptions for governance. The ACG fulfills an important role as a framework; however, much needs to be done to arrive at a specific corporate governance strategy. This leap from framework to policies and practices of a company is significant and the guidance to navigate from the framework to a governance plan is at best vague and negligible. It is likely that governance principles were derived in isolation of or without considering a framework. For example, it is difficult to ascertain whether a specific principle, say, director independence, is borne out of a governance framework. It appears that the most commonly suggested principles, such as the requirement of independence, are identifiable with agency theory rather than the ACG framework.

There are, however, parts of the ACG framework that apply toward the articulation and execution of governance. For example, the concept of requisite variety is clearly related to the design of effective internal controls. The lack of attention to the need for requisite variety could result in controls with significant deficiency and thus could cause more problems instead of mitigating targeted risk. Nevertheless, the ACG does not translate into prescriptions; however, it may allow one to identify certain principles. Arguably as a bridge to principles of corporate governance, the ACG framework is not helpful in charting specific actions.

Considerable discussion ensues in the literature regarding the goals and objectives of governance and the corresponding board role, which can be described in bipolar form as (1) compliance or (2) performance, that is, (1) the company's ability to comply with applicable laws, rules, and regulations and (2) the company's capacity to achieve performance goals. It seems the ACG framework is targeted more at the performance objective rather than compliance. In directing and controlling performance, the context is central to the task and each company's plan of action would likely be unique. A comparison across companies on performance is far more difficult than a determination of compliance. The real world of governance seems to overweight the compliance requirements. Of course, even an exceptional level of performance may not be worth much if the compliance requirements are not met.

Finally, it is important to note that in practice, two approaches to governance are common: principles or prescriptions. In some regions of the world, the corporations are asked to follow the principles and explain if they deviate from them in practice. This places a much greater burden of proof on those in charge of governance; they cannot hide behind any rules. In contrast, some other regions set the governance requirements in the form of rules. In the USA, compliance with set rules dominates the minds of directors. Such compliance is considered satisfactory, but may not result in effective governance of the company. While rules make things simple, they do not necessarily result in adherence to the spirit of governance. Since one size does not fit all, setting rules that apply across the universe of companies makes little sense; it gets easier to monitor, but it does not get easier to produce results! A holistic governance requires customization of directing and controlling actions to the company's needs.

GOVERNANCE PRINCIPLES

Several authoritative bodies have attempted to pronounce their own sets of governance principles. It is important to understand the meaning and significance of each principle, which may be more fully possible if the methods used to derive the principles was discussed in the literature for the benefit of those interested in the field. The reason why a particular principle was promulgated brings conviction and a greater degree of trust in the principle. Often, however, the discussion of groundwork that lays out the principles is minimal or missing.

OECD Principles

The Organization for Economic Cooperation and Development developed a set of corporate governance principles (see Table 2.2). Ensuring the basis for an effective corporate governance is central to the deployment of all other principles. A key beneficiary of the governance efforts is the shareholders, who must be treated equitably, without bias and with complete transparency. Stakeholders are recognized as role players in the company governance and may in turn benefit from the company's governance. Due to the information asymmetry between the company and its owners, disclosure and transparency are important pillars of communication with shareholders. Finally, the board of directors forms the hub of company governance, so it is important to articulate responsibilities of the board.

NACD Principles

The National Association of Corporate Directors (NACD) narrowly focuses on the governance principles with a view to guide directors on their duty to direct and control the company. As a result, the first principle in the NACD list is the final principle in the OECD list. Table 2.3 lists the NACD principles. The remaining nine principles in the NACD list essentially articulate the board's qualifications and role in governance. Principles 3, 4, 5, and 6 point to the director competencies, skills, and requirements of integrity, ethics, and independence. Principle 9 addresses the need for shareholder input in director selection, usually facilitated through proxy votes and sometimes shareholder proposals.

TABLE 2.2 OECD principles

1. Ensuring the basis for an effective corporate governance framework

2. The rights of shareholders and key ownership functions

3. The equitable treatment of shareholders

4. The role of stakeholders in corporate governance

5. Disclosure and transparency

6. The responsibilities of the board

TABLE 2.3 NACD principles

1. Board responsibility for governance

2. Corporate governance transparency

3. Director competency and commitment

4. Board accountability and objectivity

5. Independent board leadership

6. Integrity, ethics, and responsibility

7. Attention to information, agenda, and strategy

8. Protection against board entrenchment

9. Shareholder input in director selection

10. Shareholder communication

Principles 3 and 10 refer to disclosure and transparency in communication with shareholders. Principle 9 draws attention to the execution of corporate governance measures through the dissemination and discussion of relevant information, deliberate agenda setting to achieve effective governance, and assistance in and monitoring of execution of the company strategy.

Table 2.4 presents a comparative view of the OECD and NACD principles. The former is a high-level view of corporate governance, while the latter is a distillation of broad principles in terms of what they mean to company directors and the board. The OECD list does not include director qualifications, for these are relatively granular and focused on the director roles only. The NACD principles omit fair treatment of shareholders and recognition of the role of stakeholders in governance, perhaps because these are assumed in the development of specific board-related aspects of governance. In sum, it is fair to say that NACD articulation of board-specific principles are nested in the OECD principles.

TABLE 2.4 A comparison of OECD and NACD principles

Classification	OECD principle	NACD principle
Framework or parts of it	Ensuring the basis for an effective corporate governance framework	Protection against board entrenchment
Shareholder rights and duties	The rights of shareholders and key ownership functions	Shareholder input in director selection
Fairness	The equitable treatment of shareholders	
Information asymmetry	Disclosure and transparency	Corporate governance transparency Shareholder communication
Stakeholder roles	The role of stakeholders in corporate governance	
Director qualifications		Director competency and commitment Independent board leadership Integrity, ethics, and responsibility
Board duties	The responsibilities of the board	Board responsibility for governance Board accountability and objectivity Attention to information, agenda, and strategy

Transparency

Included in the discussion above is a relatively rarely encountered concept of transparency. Intuitively, it makes general sense but the specificity of the concept and how it plays out in practice is unclear. Table 2.5 provides a brief discussion of the concept.

FRAMEWORKS AND PRINCIPLES IN REGULATION

It is difficult to say whether lawmakers and government enforcement agencies, such as the SEC, pay attention to frameworks, principles, or research studies in the area of corporate governance and their likely role in crafting legislation. They probably do. And yet, in the process of

TABLE 2.5 The concept of transparency.

The meaning of the multidimensional, umbrella term "transparency" is unclear.
According to Michener and Bersch (2011), the scholarly exuberance in research pursuits
concerning transparency have not been underpinned by any collective understanding of
"transparency," much less any debate on what constitutes transparency, what does not,
and how to go about assessing its quality. Therefore, the role of transparency remains
opaque and potentially results in organizations' and individuals' failure to be effective,
despite possible good intentions.

The vagueness of the concept causes uncertainty in developing a sound approach to
addressing important questions. For example, how should Yum Brands have
communicated the Chinese government's launch of an investigation of allegedly
improper antibiotics used by suppliers of chicken to their KFC business unit in China?
How much information regarding the health of Steve Jobs should have been revealed by
Apple Corporation when he took an indefinite leave of absence from the company's CEO
position? Barring a few exceptions, it is hard to argue against being transparent. And yet,
it seems impossible to stake a claim of being transparent.

Transparency touches deeply on the following three dimensions:

- Openness (*honesty*): Openness involves judgments about what it is that would
  affect the stakeholder's decisions and its consideration about content to be
  disclosed. Information must be reasonably complete and found with relative ease
  and must facilitate inference.
- Communication: *adequate* and *timely* communication in order for the stakeholder to benefit from information on hand.
- Accountability: information that is disclosed is *reliable* and a *truthful representation* of reality.

Lainie Petersen (2008) extends the scope of true transparency beyond what we do and
into the domain of who we are. The intention here is to define transparency as
intrinsic, not just a behavioral phenomenon. You can't be transparent to the outside
world and not be transparent internally (to yourself), for it has to do with "who we
are," not just "what we do." Thus, clarity in the practice of transparency could lead to
a code of conduct based on ethical precepts.

Weber (2008, p. 344) asserts that transparency is seen as an important component of good
governance. But Michener and Bersch (2011) conclude that transparency is used as a means
of describing, not explaining, and this has resulted in a rainbow of meanings assigned to the
term *transparency*. It seems that a large degree of variance characterizes the meaning of the
term.

Normally, transparency enhancements depend on "the purposes for which information
is sought, the capacity and incentives of actors to provide that information, and the

(Continued)

TABLE 2.5 (Cont.)

strategies adopted to foster transparency" (Mitchell, 1998, pp. 109–110). Weber (2008, p. 344) differentiates between procedural, decision-making, and substantive transparency, and Heald (2006, pp. 27–28) proposes directions of transparency (upward, downward, outward, and inward).

With improved understanding of transparency, it would be feasible to sharpen the language of code of conduct, improve employee training, write more effective policies, and communicate effectively with stakeholders.

Adapted from: Raval, V. and Draehn, R. L. 2019. Transparency in Corporate Governance: A Bibliometric Mapping of the Concept and Related Terms, a working paper, Creighton University.

introducing a bill, lawmakers do not seem to publicly disclose what might shed light on why certain provisions were enacted and what consequences, if any, they would have on effective corporate governance. For example, one regulation regarding executive compensation has to do with disclosure of pay ratio – the ratio of the CEO compensation to the median wage of employees in the company. While this statistic may be exciting or politically appealing, it does little to enhance governance. There may be a number of reasons why this ratio may be high or low compared to the company's peers. Much of change in regulatory requirements seems driven by political motives, such as appeasing one's constituency, rather than framing a logically sound and holistic body of legislation. If laws and regulations were perfect, we wouldn't see so many corporate frauds.

A similar argument can be made regarding recent trends toward the rollback of regulations. Again, it is not clear if such rollbacks are heuristically identified or analytically traced to determine if their value is less than what it costs to comply. In some cases, it may be difficult to isolate the cost-effectiveness of a single regulation since the regulation may be working in consonance with other related provisions.

Finally, the laws and regulations address only the conformance, not performance, requirements. It is perhaps obvious that one cannot regulate company performance. However, this slant in regulation could give a wrong impression that all that effective corporate governance entails is compliance. If anything, to achieve best possible results for the shareholders is equally important for the company.

Principles and Best Practices

Over time, lessons learned from the field combined with research findings have generated voluminous data on corporate governance mechanisms. To the extent that such findings are not part of regulations, the message is considered as the best practice rather than a principle. Best practices are not a requirement and therefore may not be adopted by the responsible party, such as the board, in its governance of the company. Arguably, the difference between principle and best practice centers on the specific context of the company. A principle is in the spirit of a mandate, while a best practice is one that is best suited to a specific firm. Consequently, best practice has to be considered on a case-by-case basis, while principles apply across the board without regard to the contextual circumstances of the company.

Because companies operate in their own, unique way, it is difficult to frame some of the best practices into principles. For example, how the firm chooses its organization structure, what business model it adopts, what business strategy it selects, what risk mitigation approach it decides to implement, and how the firm positions itself to cope with uncertainty – these are questions uniquely addressed by each firm. This sort of custo- mization is difficult to carve into a principle, although theories and paradigms are available for the firm to use in such decision making.

An example of best practice is that the board chair should be a person separate from the one who serves as the CEO of the same company. Often, in evaluating whether a best practice could be viable without any negative consequences, individual case facts may make a difference, requiring judgment as to what path to take. However, handing the two very power- ful roles to one person creates a major single point of failure. For example, management overrides of control become more probable as separation of duties at the very top of the hierarchy is ignored. Conceptually, one could ask: how could the CEO who represents management be allowed to represent shareholders also? Perception today is that in some cases, the separation of the board chair from the CEO could negatively impact the company and its performance. This may be because the chairman is also founder of the business who envisioned the opportunity and created a thriving company by implementing the vision. For instance, could Tesla be the same without its visionary, Elon Musk? It is highly unlikely.

Given such scenarios, the separation of the board chair and the CEO is suggested as only a best practice and not a principle.

Principles generally are cornerstones of governance, and therefore cannot be disregarded in governance decisions, although they likely do not have the power of the law. As empirical evidence converges and experience signals that a best practice is probably a sound thing to follow by everyone, it likely would convert into a principle and may even be considered for inclusion in the law or regulation. For example, in the matter of chairman and CEO roles, the SEC now requires companies to disclose in their proxy statement whether the two roles are combined and the reason for choosing to do so.

Principles or Prescriptions?

Conceptually, there are two ways to seek compliance: rely on integrity (principles driven) or spell out the rules (compliance driven). The former emphasizes that integrity is reflected in principles defined to guide behavior; the latter considers compliance as conformance to rules that suggest satisfactory behavior. Most legal mandates lead to specific requirements or rules; besides, the organization may set its own additional rules of behavior. The integrity approach requires that the overall tone of conduct is set for the firm and, from this, compliance will follow. The integrity-based approach should meet the legal requirements, but may even rise above such dictates.

It is easy to understand why compliance in a strictly legal sense matters. If the laws and regulations are not complied with, enforcement actions from government agencies, including the SEC, may trigger. Mired in the enforcement actions, management may not be able to give its full attention to the real business on hand. Thus, company performance slips while the cleanup from noncompliance takes priority. Legal compliance is thus the lowest common denominator of any governance. Without it, the company will have difficulty surviving.

A rules-based approach makes it easier to defend the firm's actions and thus is a convenient way to justify what is done. However, too much reliance on rules may create the tone of legal absolutism. Satisfactory implementation of rules would increase the cost of doing business and may even marginalize the essence of good governance. A principles-driven approach requires that the actions are defined by what is essential for corporate governance. Compared to a rules-based approach, it is a higher order solution. However, the challenge is in having members of the firm learn how to effectively translate principles into appropriate actions.

The actions that result in compliance may not result in operational performance; for example, it may not increase revenues or decrease employee turnover. Compliance invokes the thoughts of having costs, but little value in return. In contrast, the organization's tone at the top, the code of conduct and how it is implemented, and the clarity in how ethical lapses are treated – these are the actions that speak louder and set the firm on a more robust path. Without integrity in the leadership that percolates through every layer of corporate hierarchy, the focus may simply turn to asking what is expected and then delivering just that.

Rules are, or should be, drawn from what is the right thing to do. However, a rule may drift from the spirit behind it, rendering it irrelevant and valueless. Besides, complex systems, by nature, are difficult to administer using rules. Therefore, actions that are grounded in ethical principles are preferred since no predefined rule is followed; thus, the energy is focused on the right thing to do. Compared to a rules-based approach, the integrity-driven approach sits on higher grounds and likely delivers compliance as a principled exercise.

The two approaches are not mutually exclusive. In fact, compliance could be meaningfully achieved if both approaches – rules and principles – are combined in the best possible way. In the long run, this should lower the compliance costs and put the organization on a more reliable path.

Role of Regulation and Regulatory Authorities

Laws and regulations provide the lowest common denominator for the actions of the company and its management. To survive, the requirements promulgated under these laws and regulations must be met. Both laws of the state in which a company is incorporated and the federal laws apply. Broadly, the applicable state laws concern the requirements for incorporation, while the federal laws pertain to the governance of all U.S. corporations. Moreover, the requirements of the stock exchange where the securities of the company are traded comprise another set of rules, which often are congruent with the state and federal laws and the SEC regulatory requirements. The discussion of laws and regulations is embedded in the coverage of different topics throughout the book.

Underpinning Governance

A large majority of precepts are derived from the foundations of governance. Without an understanding of foundations of corporate governance, it would be difficult to grasp why certain requirements exist and how they fit in the overall picture. Therefore, this early chapter in the book provides a foundation for the comprehension of specific governance requirements discussed in the remaining chapters.

BIBLIOGRAPHY

Arjoon, S. 2006. Striking a balance between rules and principles-based approaches for effective governance: A risks-based approach. *Journal of Business Ethics* 68: 53–82.

Baker, H. K. and Anderson, R. 2010. *Corporate Governance: A Synthesis of Theory, Research, and Practice.* Hoboken, NJ: John Wiley & Sons.

de Kluyver, C. A. 2013. *A Primer on Corporate Governance*, Second Edition. New York: Business Expert Press.

Galbraith, J. R. 1974. Organization design: An information processing view. *Interfaces* 4(3): 28–36.

Heald, D. 2006. Varieties of transparency, in Hood, D. and Heald, D. (Eds.), *Transparency: The Key to Better Governance?* Oxford: Oxford University Press, pp. 25–43.

Henriques, A. and Richardson, J. (Eds.). 2013. *The Triple Bottom Line: Does It All Add Up?* eBook Edition. London: Routledge.

Michener, G. and Bersch, K. 2011. Conceptualizing the quality of transparency. *1st Global Conference on Transparency*, 17–21 May. Rutgers University, Newark, NJ.

Mitchell, R. B. 1998. Sources of transparency: Information systems in international regimes. *International Studies Quarterly* 42: 109–130.

Petersen, L. 2008. *Headspace by Lainie Petersen.* [online], www.lainiepetersen.com, Accessed October 17, 2012.

Raval, V. and Draehn, R. L. 2019. Transparency in corporate governance: A bibliometric mapping of the concept and related terms, a working paper, Creighton University.

Raval, V. and Shah, S. 2017. Third party risk management. *ISACA Journal* 2: 14–19.

Solomon, J. 2007. *Corporate Governance and Accountability*, Second Edition. Hoboken, NJ: John Wiley & Sons.

Weber, R. H. 2008. Transparency and the governance of the internet. *Computer Law & Security Report* 24(4): 342–348.

CHAPTER 3

Governance and Risk

Undeniably, risk and opportunity go together; they have no separate existence. Without taking risk, you cannot avail of the related opportunity; without entertaining an opportunity, you may be able to avoid the attendant risks. For example, if a company is considering providing its key executives with a company-owned credit card, the benefits would include streamlining of procurement of goods and services, better reporting, and more efficient transaction authorization and processing. On the other hand, the risks include loss or theft of the card and consequent fraud, misuse of the card by an authorized employee, or inappropriate accounting and justification for credit card charges. Even this relatively simple scenario shows the interplay between risk and opportunity.

UNDERSTANDING RISK

Before you avail of an opportunity, you need to identify as exhaustively as possible risk exposures stemming from the opportunity; specifically, the probability that the risk would materialize and as a result, the dollar amount of loss you would incur. Past experience alone may not be sufficient to inventory all possible risks and their impact. Warren Buffett, CEO of Berkshire Hathaway, talks about how the company's mistake of focusing on experience, rather than exposure, resulted in assuming a huge terrorism risk in its insurance business, for which the company received no premium. A thorough search for risks assumed is a necessary first step toward risk management.

One might think that if you don't take any action, you could avoid the attendant risk. While this may be true in the short run, the consequences of not taking action could be devastating. For example, at one time, Borders bookstore was thriving, but it took no steps to address in its strategy the upcoming digital revolution and online marketing of books and other merchandise. Consequently, competitors such as Amazon took over the market previously dominated by Borders. In today's fast-paced, dynamic business environment, disruptive technologies could easily ruin a thriving business.

Foregoing an opportunity could mean that you are creating new or different risks. If a company is not poised to exploit a specific strategic opportunity that has a good fit with the organization, chances are that someone else will embrace the idea and emerge as a formidable competitor to the company. Ignoring known risks could create new risks for the entity. Thus, status quo is not a good choice in risk management. If choices must be made in the interests of the owners, such as shareholders, it is important to consider that the risks the firm takes on are in line with the risk appetite of the owners and that such risks are appropriately mitigated while leveraging the opportunity.

Operational, Strategic, and Tactical Risks

While the relationship between risk and opportunity (or reward) is like two sides of the same coin, in practice there is a tendency to treat each separately. When risks are addressed, opportunities are not explicitly considered, for they are assumed to have been entertained. Once an opportunity is availed of, it is likely that attendant risks will then be identified and controls to mitigate the risks will be put in place.

It appears organizations take better care of existing risks than evolving risks. What is familiar to you lends itself well to risk management with ease. Risks of an occasional merger are not as easy to identify and address as the risks of mature business processes. And yet, it is the occasional merger that could prove to be a high strategic risk with significant consequences. What you know you know is easier to manage than what you don't know you don't know. Thus, risk management of existing operations is perhaps less demanding than the risk management of strategic actions. Operations and related supply chains mature over time, employees become familiar with the processes and presumably make fewer errors, and unique situations of compromise may become rare. Most controls that mitigate risks in the existing business model are likely in place and may have been tested for their effectiveness periodically. The auditors review existing controls fairly frequently and suggest corrective actions where appropriate.

The case of non-routine tactical or strategic actions is quite different. In such cases, the hindsight of experience may be absent. Consequently, the risk managers may have to wrestle with "what you don't know you don't know." Returning to the example of a merger, which presents a strategic risk rather than an operational risk, the board should insist on a risk assessment and where risks appear to be material, even a risk audit by the internal audit function or outside experts. Some years ago, Hewlett-Packard acquired a U.K.-based company for several billion dollars only to find within months that their decision to acquire was based on fraudulent data supplied by the target company's executive. Once this is known, the write off of goodwill purchased and the lawsuits to recover the investment from the fraudsters become a drain on the company. Whereas the audit committee of the board deliberates on the effectiveness of existing internal control systems regularly, it should also demand a review of the risk management plan concerning the company's business strategy.

Regulatory Compliance and Risk

Unfortunately, the word compliance triggers the thought of doing the minimum and at the least cost. Because managing risk is fundamental to shareholder interests, compliance requirements are mostly geared to control of the company. When this view is emphasized, the other side of risk – opportunity that is availed of – is underweighted. As a result, risk management as equated with compliance becomes only a question of efficiency and cost, not value. Besides, effective risk management could cause the company to avoid mishaps, the benefits of which go unnoticed. The only thing that shows up is the cost of controls, giving a biased view of risk management. For example, some companies dealt with the Y2K problem – the problem of expanding the two-digit field for the year to four digits – in a rigorous manner, and when the year 2000 unfolded, the absence of any mishaps – call it a non-event – was unfortunately touted as an endeavor that took a disproportionate amount of resources. How do you know that you are overspending in managing a particular risk? Another scenario that illustrates the point is that of disaster recovery and contingency planning, where costs come to focus in the discussion more than value. While recurring costs of continuity planning are "real" and significant each year, the benefit of such costs may never become visible. Although this may be good news overall, the CEO might ask: why throw away sizable amount of resources when nothing is happening year-after-year? Overdoing the risk mitigation is a concern as there is no limit to the amount of resources poured into the risk mitigation measures. Where do you stop in gaining more and more control over the risk?

While risk management emphasizes cost minimization with optimal results, opportunity management centers on value creation. The intense focus on growing value is clear in the mindset of startups; they do not seem to care as much about compliance, except as a necessary evil. The point is, regardless of the lifecycle stage of the company, benefits of the risk management exercise should percolate into improvements in the control processes, more effective dealing with the risks, and more efficient business processes. Importantly, the big question remains: how do you motivate the company leadership to leverage the current knowledge, technologies and data to do a better job of risk-based strategy formulation and implementation?

RISK AND UNCERTAINTY

Risk is positively associated with uncertainty, which is evident in volatility or fluctuations. Sometimes, the terms "uncertainty" and "risk" are used as synonyms. For example, VIX, the volatility index, measures the volatility of the stock market prices, with greater fluctuations reflecting higher volatility and therefore greater risk or uncertainty. Measuring the impact of any risk is a product of the probability of risk materializing into an actual event and the impact of the risk event. Both are important to consider: a skewed picture will emerge if only one factor is considered. For example, in auto insurance marketing commercials, making the viewer aware of the risk dominates the scenario – so called mayhems – with very little said about the probability of such a risk. What are the chances that a moose will break into your Texas house? This is important to consider when buying coverage; if the probability is low, then the loss would be miniscule even when the impact is high. So, paying attention to just one or the other factor is not enough; both must be considered concurrently. In today's data-driven businesses, considerable detailed analysis goes into the decisions on risk mitigation measures. Tools such as heatmaps and dashboards are available to view the results in an interactive fashion. However, the heuristics still dominate in determining the risks identified, their probable impact, and how to mitigate such risks.

Risk Appetite and Risk Tolerance

Risk represents the possibility of a loss or harm to an entity. Such an entity can be a person, an organization, a resource, a system, or a group. There is hardly any entity that does not face some type of risk. Thus, a car driver on a snowy day runs the risk of slipping and sliding, and a pedestrian walking along a street on a cold, windy day runs the risk of catching a cold. A rope walker could fall, and a convenience store clerk could get robbed! Aside from harm to individuals, other objects may be compromised. For example, a laptop can be stolen, hackers may gain access to a network, or a thief may abscond with a car stereo from an accessible vehicle in a parking lot.

Each entity is not equally impacted by an identified risk. For example, the risk of catching influenza virus is greater among children and seniors. Thus, risk exposure is important to consider when making a risk assessment. Low or no exposure would mean that there may not be any need to address that risk. In our example of influenza, young adults may not need to take the influenza vaccine. In business, a company based in the USA with no or insignificant revenue from abroad does not have to worry about foreign currency fluctuations relative to the U.S. dollar.

Risk appetite, as the name suggests, has to do with how much risk an entity can "stomach." In a governance context, risk appetite is a high-level understanding between management and the board about drivers of, and parameters around, opportunity-seeking behavior. It is a strategic viewpoint in guiding the organization to be disciplined in choosing, or avoiding, risks. When a business avails of an opportunity, as in acquiring a new business, the risk inherent in the acquisition would cause a degree of variability in the company performance. A company should accept those risks that are reasonable to undertake in light of the opportunity and can be effectively managed.

Risk tolerance is tactical in nature as it addresses the risk in relation to the organization's objectives. Risk tolerance is often expressed as the ability to accept volatility in performance. As an investor in financial markets, for example, the investor might find uncomfortable unusually large swings in the market valuations. So, the idea is to create a portfolio of investments that the individual would be comfortable in experiencing swings in the performance of the portfolio. Similarly, a corporation should keep its business segments within a tolerable range of performance. Risk tolerance is likely to change over time; as the company matures, it may be able to tolerate less volatility; startups, on the other hand, can live with much greater swings in their destiny.

The board should periodically engage in a dialogue regarding management's appetite for risk and whether management's risk appetite is consistent with the risk profile. Since risk appetite changes as management makes key decisions, it is necessary for the board to ask: is the risk profile still congruent with the risk appetite? While these are high-level assessments with significant subjective judgments, any discussion that would lead to a better understanding of management's risk profile and risk appetite should prove helpful in the governance of the company.

RISK MANAGEMENT APPROACHES

Risk management involves mitigation of the potential adverse effects of risk. In reality, one needs to manage the risk that one owns or accepts through choices made. Any risk that is dis-owned does not require risk mitigation. If a soccer coach chooses to travel by train or car only, and not by air, the coach is able to avoid the risks of flying, such as possible mid-air collision, pilot error, or crash due to inclement weather. Since the related opportunity is abandoned when a risk is avoided, there is a possibility that others may avail of opportunity along with attendant risks and create a competitive edge of the entity that chose to seize the opportunity and take the risk. For example, if a computer outsourcing company does not engage in providing cloud computing services, sooner or later, it may find itself at a competitive disadvantage that might be hard to recover from.

Any risk that an entity assumes could be managed in various ways. A first step might be to reduce the risk. For example, the risk of hacker attacks on the organization's systems can be reduced by hardening the system against such attacks. Since computer hacks might happen due to remaining known but unaddressed or unknown vulnerabilities in the system, the remainder of the risk can either be absorbed by the organization (that is, it will accept the loss incurred) or can be transferred or shared; for example, an insurance policy may be purchased to cover the remaining risk.

Categories of Risk

A first imperative in creating an effective risk management system is to understand qualitative distinctions between three types of risk organizations face:

- Internal risk. Risks internal to the organization and controllable.

- Strategy risk. Risks emerging from the organization's strategy.

- External risk. Risks that arise out of events outside the firm and beyond the firm's control. A common and unpredictable source of business interruptions, external risk can only be mitigated by focusing on identifying them, assessing their potential impact, and figuring out how best to mitigate their effects should they occur.

This classification illustrates that risk can be categorized from the perspective of origins of risk. Thus, there are internal risks, strategic risks, and external risks. Internal risks arise from within the entity and are largely controllable by the entity. A company that strives for managing internal risks is likely to succeed in its efforts, for much of it would be repetitive and therefore predictable. Mature processes and technologies are available to mitigate internal risks. Strategic risks emerge from the failure or success of the board and the management to develop and implement strategies that deliver expected outcomes. Failure to take on strategic opportunities and manage attendant risks would result in long-term deterioration of the company. Largely uncontrollable by the entity, external risks stem from events that arise outside of the entity. All kinds of natural calamities like a flood, fire, or an earthquake are the sources of external risks. While external risks may not be controllable, it is incumbent upon the company to innovate and implement ways in which early warning signs are generated, or the damage to human life and resources is minimized. The electric utility,

PG&E, in California has come under criticism for its lack of attention to equipment that accentuated the cause of fire and is now attempting to find ways to minimize losses from forest fires.

The board and management should provide oversight of control processes in place to manage internal risks and to mitigate the impact of external risks through disaster recovery and contingency planning. As for strategic risks, going beyond the oversight, the board may want to actively engage in strategy formulation and provide subsequent oversight of strategy implementation. While all risks must be managed, the failure to manage strategic risks can prove disastrous to the viability of the company.

COSO CONTROL FRAMEWORK

For a systematic approach to address myriad risks throughout the organization, it is necessary to adopt a risk management framework, often called a control framework. In the corporate governance arena, a control framework that is widely accepted is called COSO. The Committee of Sponsoring Organizations (COSO) of the Treadway Commission, following a recommendation of the Commission, studied the domain of internal controls in a comprehensive manner. The scope of the COSO study was quite comprehensive and resulted in an integrated framework of internal controls, called the COSO framework. This framework proposes five components of internal controls: risk assessment, control environment, control activities, information and communication, and monitoring. Together, these five components and the relationships among them make a holistic framework of internal controls, which is discussed further in Chapter 8. A noteworthy development in progressive improvement of the COSO framework is called COSO ERM (Enterprise Risk Management). ERM also addresses strategy and identifies some of the components implicit in the initial COSO framework.

Several other control frameworks have been developed over time. For example, COBIT and ISO 17,799 provide additional granularity and depth to accommodate the increasingly important role of technology, which is contributing to both emerging risks and also technology-based controls. The regulatory requirement in the USA mandates the use of any control framework, and if one is not used, requires an explanation for the non-use. Finally, the most popular control framework among the public companies has been the COSO framework.

GOVERNANCE AND RISK MANAGEMENT

A primary purpose of corporate governance is to provide oversight and direct management with a view to maximize return to the shareholders in the long run. Such returns are not automatic nor guaranteed; they are subject to risk. To ensure that best results are obtained in the interest of shareholders, risks that might limit the potential returns should be managed. Governance is thus closely tied to risk management. In fact, there would be no need for governance if there was no risk present to the achievement of returns to shareholders. The focus of governance is therefore on risk management of the enterprise. In almost every action of the board of directors, for example, what is potentially evident is the intention to limit exposure to risks and manage risks that are owned by the corporation.

At the board level, the accountability to monitor and direct risk management is often assigned to the audit committee of the board, the committee that is responsible for oversight on financial disclosure and reporting and on the controls over financial reporting. Assisting the committee is the internal audit function that provides insights on the effectiveness of internal controls and suggests improvement to the control framework.

The interaction between governance and risk management can be illustrated using the case of The Boeing Company. Following twin fatal crashes involving 737 MAX aircrafts, the company's board asked its committee to review Boeing's aircraft design and manufacturing processes with a focus on the aircraft's safety. As a result, the board acted on the following recommendations of the committee:

- Create a centralized product and services safety unit that reports to the company's chief engineer and a board-level committee that includes the company's CEO.

- Make safety-related experience a criterion for choosing future directors.

- Restructure the reporting responsibility of the design engineers, who currently report to business managers, directly to the top management.

In addition to acting on the recommendations above, the board also expanded the whistleblower system to include explicitly the reporting by employees of any concerns related to safety and reinforced the role of the safety review board at the company level.

The first recommendation sends the signal to the company employees and other stakeholders that safety is a top priority. It resets the tone-from-the-top and calibrates the company culture to attend to safety. The second suggestion would change the mix of the board members in terms of sensitivity to safety. In the long run, with more directors experienced in safety issues, oversight and control of management actions will be more heavily weighted by concerns for safety. This in turn could help avoid catastrophes experienced with 737 MAX 8 aircraft. The third step would reduce the time-to-market pressures presumably coming from business managers, allowing the engineers to ensure that safety is fully addressed in the decision to roll out products and services. Overall, this vividly illustrates the role of governance in risk management. Practically every step that the board and other regulators consider taking is colored by the question of risk, how it would change, and what will be done to manage the risk.

BIBLIOGRAPHY

Buffett, W. 2001. Letter to shareholders. https://www.berkshirehathaway.com/letters/letters.html, Accessed Jan. 21, 2020.

Cameron, D. 2019. Boeing centralizes safety oversight. *The Wall Street Journal,* October 1, B3.

Kaplan, R. S. and Mikes, A. 2012. Managing risks: A new framework. *Harvard Business Review* June 2012 48–60.

Protiviti. 2010. Board perspectives: Risk oversight. *The Risk Appetite Dialogue* 50(4).

Raval, V. and Fichadia, A. 2007. *Risks, Controls, and Security: Concepts and Applications.* New York: John Wiley & Sons.

Viscelli, T. R., Hermanson, D. R. and Beasley, M. S. 2017. The integration of ERM and strategy: Implications for corporate governance. *Accounting Horizons* 31(2): 69–82.

CHAPTER 4

Ethical Dimensions of Corporate Governance

C. S. Lewis, an intellectual giant of the 20th century, asserted that moral rules are directions for running the human machine. These directions have three purposes: to keep our own internal engines running smoothly, to keep our communities in harmony, and to help us follow the general purpose of human life as a whole. We face moral questions in four roles: as a person, as an economic agent, as a company leader, and beyond a firm's boundaries. Work as such probably existed ever since the origin of human being; however, the degree of structure given to it came about only later. Progressively over time, as the groups, ventures, and trades became more formalized, the identity of the firm separate from its participants became more vivid. The issues of the group took shape as uniquely those of the group and their moral treatment grew into a separate domain.

Over the past centuries, advances in business organizations have led to the recognition of business as an entity separate from its shareholders. As businesses grow and become more complex, global entities, this separation becomes increasingly sophisticated and consequently, the issues of morality weigh in heavily. The challenge may be quite broad, from choosing a business mission, to consciously struggling with a business model, to adopting a strategy that is morally appropriate. Take, for example, Ashley Madison's slogan: "Life is short. Have an affair." This borders on the virtualization of some of the morally unacceptable indulgences. Sadly, the mission weaves into the moral fabric of the firm, leaving the company no choice but to rationalize possible indiscretions it may nurture. On the other hand, legitimate businesses such as Facebook have run into a continuous struggle to prove what appears to be genuine intention of protecting the privacy of its patrons. It has not been an easy ride for Facebook or Google on the privacy front, presumably despite their best intentions. In contrast, transgressions at Volkswagen, although huge and unforgivable, are probably a one-off actualization of the temptation to cheat. Whether the company is able to address issues of this nature and correct itself going forward is largely dependent on tone *from* the top, discussed later.

As work and private life take distinct boundaries, it is clear that morality of the business entity would need to be addressed as a separate realm. While one's moral precepts stay the same when entering the employer's door, how these will play into a complex group environment remains a puzzle. A great deal depends upon the organization and its leadership in laying the foundation to help insiders determine what is right and what is wrong.

CONCEPTUAL FOUNDATIONS

In dealing with the ethics of business firms, Freeman's separation thesis offers a fair warning. The thesis says that people tend to treat an issue as a business decision distinctly separate from the same issue as a moral decision. Perhaps the comfort level of the decision maker is high when the two are dealt with separately. It is likely that accountability for the business decision is clear and distinct from the accountability for ethical considerations for the same decision. However, in as much as this makes the exercise less messy, the discreteness both simplifies and marginalizes the uncertainty and fuzziness of ethics. The twin disasters of Boeing's 737 MAX aircraft in 2019 serve as an example. It is likely that the pressure to rollout the jets – a business decision – caused the managers to assume that the safety issues – a moral imperative – were adequately addressed. Unfortunately, it appears this was not true. Ethical questions of the traveler's safety stayed in the background while the business decision to launch the jets took precedence.

Perhaps it was easier in the distant past to separate a business decision from its ethical side. The invention of the wheel or the printing press in all likelihood did not entail at the outset questions of ethics, questions that become pronounced only when the technology is applied in the real world. But this is not feasible in most situations anymore.

A business decision has ethical consequences and addressing such consequences could result in a reconsideration of the decision. For example, the privacy consideration of patrons' data would remain inherently tied with Facebook's decisions to leverage such data for its revenue generation. The scrimmage between patrons' privacy rights and the desire to bring people together on a given platform will continue for Facebook throughout its existence.

Ogburn's cultural lag thesis reinforces potential consequences of Freeman's separation theory. Essentially, Ogburn argues that material culture advances more rapidly than nonmaterial culture. The material culture pushes accomplishments on the visible worldly progress rewarded by its vested interests. The nonmaterial culture has to do with morality, an existential exercise. According to Ogburn, the material culture advances at a much faster rate than the nonmaterial culture. As a result, there exists a time gap between the material and nonmaterial cultures. Moreover, there exists a gap in the state of advancement of each culture at any point in time, suggesting an alignment gap. The plausible inference is that one might think moral issues can wait while material progress must continue. In part, this may have been exacerbated by the rewards aligned more heavily with material progress. Figure 4.1 presents an interpretation of Ogburn's cultural lag thesis.

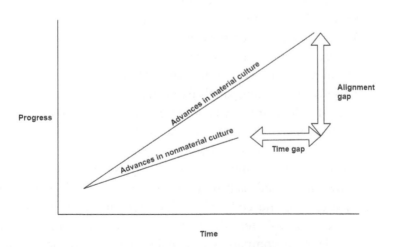

FIGURE 4.1   An interpretation of Ogburn's cultural lag thesis.

Both alignment gap and time gap could be significant and visible in the case of large startups. With the glut of venture capital tempted to yield mega returns on its commitment to a startup, the up and coming businesses get relatively easy access to capital. At the same time, the sources of capital, such as venture capital firms, may be more forgiving, or lax, toward the startup's conduct of business, giving unchecked control to the founder. The entrepreneur CEO takes the business reins in her hands and has a free-wheeling ride as long as revenues keep growing and competition, both traditional and innovative, is challenged. Generally, startups are too busy growing their business, with very little time to address the nonmaterial culture, which may remain vague and perhaps even unidentified. The emphasis on value-centered behavior may not come up in creating an ethically appropriate culture. Arguably, there is no time for it! The governance of the startup could thus be loose and undisciplined.

The case of We Company, the parent of WeWork, a space-sharing company that subleases office space to businesses, illustrates the point. The company in mid-2019 made a failed attempt to launch an initial public offering (IPO). Several reasons contributed to this outcome. First, the revenue growth was not leading to smaller losses, or profits; instead, the company continued to make very large losses. The private investors grew leery about the valuation of the company around the IPO launch, which started at $47 billion and eventually shrank to $15 billion. The leadership style of the entrepreneur, CEO and chairman of the board, Adam Neumann, came under scrutiny. His substantial loans from the company to buy the company's shares was seen as a conflict of interest stemming from a related-party transaction. He also sold for $6 million the right to use WE in the company's name; however, this transaction was later reversed. Mr. Neumann's wife, Rebekah, was a co-founder and chief brand and impact officer and also was the CEO of the company's private elementary school. Mr. Neumann had ownership interests in some of the properties leased by the company. Collectively, such actions mirrored ineffective governance and lack of value-centered leadership. Although organizational culture and code of conduct may appear to be soft and indirect in a company's life, ethical grounding of the company plays a significant role in the company's sustainable growth in the long run. In

We Company's case, it appears both the alignment gap and the time gap turned out to be impactful in investors' decisions.

What, then, is the remedy to bring balance back in the life of a corporation? At the highest level, policies are an effective way to set the stage for what is acceptable and what will likely be considered outright wrong. While policies cannot spell out every single incident, individually and collectively, the organization's policies build a cohesive footprint for expected behavior. One of the key documents that echoes the company's moral grounding is the code of conduct policy. Sections 406 and 407 of the Sarbanes Oxley Act (SOX) led to a statutory requirement that a public company should disclose if it has adopted a code of ethics and if not, it must explain why. The code should apply to the board members, the management, and employees of the company. The company must also disclose changes in, and waivers from the code of ethics.

CODE OF CONDUCT

The code of conduct sets the tone, the ways in which the organization is expected to behave. Since the organization is a group of people, the code essentially is addressed to people involved in the organization: directors, senior management, executives, and other employees – people responsible for abiding by the code. There are no exceptions. Only the board may approve of any exceptions for any executive and this, too, should be in a transparent manner; proper disclosure of approved exceptions is necessary.

In the USA, public companies must adopt a code. It is a regulatory requirement that cannot be ignored; companies that fail to adopt a code must disclose the fact that they do not have a code, adding reasons why that is the case. Aspirational in nature, the code's message is positively coined. The code normally links the company's mission and values to expected conduct; often, it includes examples of how the linkage from mission and values to day-to-day decision-making translates for the employees.

As evident in codes of various companies (e.g., Google, Microsoft), there is considerable flexibility in content and its delivery. Some firms choose to have two codes of conduct, one for directors and management, and the other for employees. Where separate codes exist, the difference may be in emphasis; for example, the former assumes much greater influence on the part of directors and managers for whom some situations – such as conflict of interest – are more likely to arise and should be specifically addressed in the code. Often set in a conversational tone, the employee code punctuates each employee's responsibility for the conduct as an individual, in a group setting, and while serving others both within and outside the company. Content should emphasize ethical and value-centered behavior and encourage convergence with the company's mission and goals. It must include noticeable conflicts, such as bribery, gifts, and other accommodations granted to fellow employees, customers, suppliers and service providers, regulators, and representatives of the government. Added to these are privacy and confidentiality, data and information protection, and respect for others' rights. Some of these are clearly identified as compliance requirements under the current laws and regulations. Table 4.1 summarizes typical content of a code of conduct.

TABLE 4.1 Code of conduct – an illustrative content outline.

A. Purpose and expectations

 Compliance with applicable laws

 Adherence to ethical standards

 Conflict-free behavior in the best interests of the company

B. Key company policies (examples)

 Protection of corporate assets

 Confidentiality

 Technology – acceptable use

 Fraud of corporate assets

 Conflict of interest (examples)

 Interests in other businesses

 Outside activities during business hours

 Gifts and entertainment

 Working with the government (examples)

 Legal and regulatory compliance

(Continued)

TABLE 4.1 (Cont.)

Political activity and contributions

Obstruction of justice

Workplace behavior (examples)

Employee privacy

Respectful work environment

Personal use of corporate assets

C. Compliance, guidance and reporting

Compliance reporting responsibility of the employee

Reporting questionable activity

Reporting misconduct

Contact information for questions and help

Enforcement of the code

Corporations are more likely to have their own customized code of ethics, for a "vanilla" version fails to address specific challenges of moral accountability. For example, Union Pacific Railroad remarkably stresses the importance of safety and mandates norms for the practice of safety throughout the organization. Pacific Gas and Electric Company, a California utility, also emphasizes safety of its stakeholders, although it unfortunately has a bad track record of delivering the promise of safety to the customers it serves.

It is important to include in the code whom to contact if the person has questions, encounters gray areas, or simply does not know the right way to respond. Similarly, it must include hotlines (also called whistle-blower lines) where the person can anonymously post information regarding illegal or inappropriate activities. Table 4.2 discusses the characteristics and benefits of whistleblower systems. Finally, those

TABLE 4.2 Whistleblower systems.

A whistleblower system is a proactive and potentially cost-effective means to use in corporate governance. It is a communication system which permits anyone to post information regarding suspicious activities, waste of resources, fraud, or abuse of policies of the corporation. Available anytime, it allows persons – by phone or through a website – to anonymously report anything they believe is in violation of the law, regulations, or company policies and the code of conduct. Anonymity is assured and the reporting person may choose to report the incident completely anonymously. In the case of an externally outsourced system, the whistleblower may have the option to remain anonymous to the company, but accessible to the outsourced system, so that additional information may be sought from the tipster, if necessary, by the provider of the system at the request of the company. Public companies are required to maintain a whistleblower system by Section 301(4) of the Sarbanes Oxley Act.

The system should be user-friendly and accessible from anywhere, including public places such as a local library. Anonymity and accessibility are the two most important requirements for the system to produce results. Without having anonymity, the tipster's risks of retribution increase significantly. Another prerequisite for a successful system is that it should be trustworthy. Without trusting the receiving end, the provider of highly sensitive information is unlikely to volunteer to participate in it. In order for the system to be viable, it is necessary that employees (and perhaps external parties such as customers and suppliers) are aware of the existence of the system, understand that the reported information is subject to anonymity, and know how to access and use it. It would help to send periodic reminders about the system, for people tend to forget what they may not have used recently or ever.

The whistleblower system is a generic obstacle to wrongdoing. It doesn't matter whether the issue has to do with inventory, sales, employee hiring or firing, or something else – regardless of the specific context, every incident is reportable to a single source, the hotline. The tips shared by people may range from perceived sex discrimination to hallucination-prompted fears of a mentally ill person, to compromise of internal controls or company policies; each tip needs to be carefully analyzed to understand the underlying issue and appropriately respond to it. All tips are important in some way to identify anomalies, correct the problem, or where there is no problem found, to at least address the perception of a problem. For those in charge of governance, the most significant tips address irregularities in management behavior, perhaps leading to misappropriation of company assets or financial reporting fraud.

The integrity of the system warrants that each and every tip received is automatically logged, with time stamp, so that it can be addressed by someone accountable for the

(Continued)

TABLE 4.2 (Cont.)

concerned domain. Automated whistleblower systems permit routing of the tip directly to the person accountable for it; for example, financial fraud tips are received by the chair of the audit committee and all other tips are directed to chief compliance officer. Upon receipt of a complaint, the system informs via email in real-time the person responsible to address it. The incident is logged in the system's database. No incident can remain on the books without a follow through within a predefined time limit. The audit committee agenda should include discussion of incidents reported and the progress toward addressing the concerns expressed. Collective intelligence gained from the incidents may help improve internal controls.

Finally, what works for public companies is equally desirable for government and nonprofit entities. The governance of any organization regardless of compliance requirements relating to whistleblower systems can benefit from its use. The Internal Revenue Service seeks tips through its hotline on tax return frauds or improprieties, and the SEC wants to know of any public company violations of regulations. These government agencies have established a reward system for the tipsters where the amount of reward is contingent upon the value of the tip.

accountable to live by the code must be offered training about the code, its interpretation, and how to abide by it.

Since people don't necessarily encounter illegal or unethical behaviors routinely, they might forget about the code's requirements. Therefore, periodic reminders are helpful in enforcing the code; where deemed appropriate, the company may also ask employees to sign a statement acknowledging that the employee has read the code of conduct.

Implementing the Code

The code is useless unless it has "teeth." Therefore, it is necessary to lay out candidly any and all possible consequences in the event of violation of the code. Generally, the approach of zero tolerance has the most force. The consequences actually dealt with speak louder than the words. However, once someone has violated the code and has been punished for it, the next violation by the same person may not be stoppable because of the addictive behavior. In such instances, the actor suffers from failure of self-regulation and progressively becomes weaker in exercising self-control. The actor might rationalize that indiscretions

TABLE 4.3 (Cont.)

better. Under such circumstances, there would be little hope that the code of conduct would deliver the expected behavior.

Subsequent to the massive forest fires presumably caused by PGE errors and omissions, the company has been inundated with lawsuits, the CPUC has been extensively investigating the company, and the company has filed for bankruptcy protection. The silver lining for governance comes from a new position of ethics and compliance officer, a nearly complete changeover of directors and the replacement of the CEO. The future of PGE is uncertain; in as much as the utility has to prevail to serve the community, it is likely that different alternatives might be explored.

MONITORING MORALITY

The code of conduct, at least on paper if not in spirit, represents the presumed character of the firm. It gives the initial mark of the firm's character, its integrity and reliability and thus, the amount of trust present and prospective investors could place in the firm and its management. The words on paper should constantly mirror in practice in order to maintain stakeholders' trust in the firm. Enron had a good code and so did Arthur Andersen, but they both vanished. The break-down in trust could occur precipitously and the firm may not be able to recover from it, and if it does recover, it will not be without significant sacrifices. The case of PG&E illustrates how vital is the code in the life of a business, and yet, how challenging it is to keep the code alive in its spirit.

It should be acknowledged that monitoring morality is no easy deal. It is more of an art than a science and much of it flows from the heart rather than the mind. However, effortful and well-intentioned attempts must be continuously made by the leaders, including directors, of the company to keep the message front and center of every undertaking the business commits to. Because ethical behavior is often not explicitly accounted for in employee behavior, it could get on a slippery slope easily, especially under pressures of achieving short-term goals. There is no better way to reinforce value-centered behavior than by expressing those values in one's own behavior. Employees learn vicariously and pattern their behavior accordingly.

BIBLIOGRAPHY

Badaracco, J. L., Jr. and Webb, A. P. 1995. Business ethics: The view from the trenches. *California Management Review* 37(2): 8–28.

Brown, E., Cimilluca, D., Benoit, D. and Farrell, M. 2019. WeWork's high-octane CEO steps down under pressure. *The Wall Street Journal*, September 25, A1, A14..

Order instituting investigation and order to show cause on the Commission's own motion into the operations and practices of Pacific Gas and Electric Company with respect to locate and mark practices and related matters. 2018. California Public Utilities Commission I.18-12-007, December 13, 2018.

PG&E Code of Conduct for Employees. 2019. www.pgecorp.com/corp/about-us/corporate-governance/corporation-policies/employee-conduct.page, Accessed September10, 2019.

Raval, V. 2012. Changing times and the eternality of ethics. *The ISACA Journal* 2.

The We Company. 2019, Form S-1 filed with the Securities and Exchange Commission. August 19. www.sec.gov/Archives/edgar/data/1533523/000119312519220499/d781982ds1.htm#toc781982_10, Accessed October 3, 2019.

II

Governance Roles and Structure

CHAPTER 5

Role Players in Corporate Governance

At first, the scenario of players in the corporate governance arena is imposing. Several diverse entities, including individuals, groups and organizations, are engaged in the process. It is therefore essential to discuss each major participant's nature and role in the governance process. A view of the players and relationships among them will help clarify governance issues, their source, and one or more parties accountable to address the issue. In this sense, this chapter provides a framework for further discussion in the remaining chapters of this book. An overview of the participants and relationships among them is shown in Figure 5.1. Each dotted line in the figure suggests an indirect, or implicit, link between the two role players.

SHAREHOLDERS, THE BOARD, AND THE MANAGEMENT

Shareholders, the board of directors, and senior management form the nucleus of the governance ecosystem. Shareholders are the principal; the directors are shareholders who represent the universe of shareholders of the company. Conceptually, directors are agents of the principal (that is, shareholders) and at the same time, principal in relation to the management, which has the role of agent in the principal-agent relationship. In the governance context, the entire management cadre is not represented; rather, only the senior management is recognized as reporting to the board and shareholders. At a minimum, senior management is

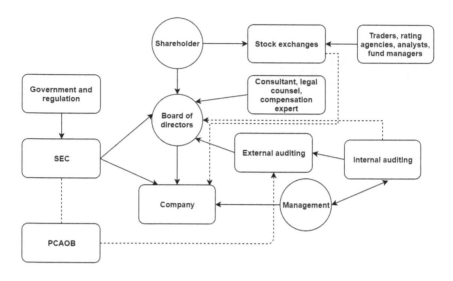

FIGURE 5.1   Role players in corporate governance.

comprised of the CEO and the CFO, and often includes the chief administrative officer, president, or chief operating officer. Often, if a non-executive director chairs the board, the CEO is elected to the board. It is likely that other top leaders of the company may also be elected to the board.

Shareholders

The term *investor* refers to any entity (individual, mutual fund, hedge fund, pension plan, etc.) that has invested in any organization using any investment vehicle or instrument (shares, bonds, loans, etc.). The term *shareholder* is more specific: it refers to the investor in shares of a particular corporation. A shareholder may own voting or non-voting shares issued by the corporation. Often in the corporate governance field, reference to shareholder is specifically linked to those who hold voting common shares in a publicly traded company.

Whether a shareholder is an organization or an individual, the identification as a shareholder begins with the point in time when shares are purchased and ends when these shares are sold. Shares may be purchased by an investor at the time the company issues the IPO, or later when the shares begin trading on the stock exchange that enlists the shares. Throughout this tenure, the shareholder is entitled to receive cash dividends, if declared by the board. Sometimes, the board may declare a stock dividend (dividend in the form of additional shares); upon receipt of the stock dividend, the number of shares owned by the shareholder will increase by the amount of the stock dividend.

During an entity's term as a shareholder, the entity is entitled to all shareholder rights to information and the right to vote on matters such as election of the board members and ratification of independent auditors. Some companies issue dual class voting shares where a separate class of shares usually has a larger number of votes assigned per share. Dual class voting shares are used to control the ownership of the company, and thereby control the decisions put forth for a vote by shareholders, or by certain interested parties, such as the founder of the business.

Shareholders are the primary beneficiaries of the governance efforts. They are the ones whose interests in the business are protected. The focus of corporate governance is on creating long term value for the shareholders. Although other stakeholders may be considered as beneficiaries of the company, most of the legal focus and regulatory enforcement revolves around monitoring any compromises that bite into shareholder interests. For example, trading of shares by a party that has sensitive information yet unreleased to the shareholders is called insider trading, which is illegal, and the violators are punished for using privileged information. Chapter 7 discusses the shareholders; Chapter 12 informs shareholder communication and engagement aspects of governance.

The Board

The responsibility for governance of the company almost entirely hinges upon the directors, elected representatives of the shareholders. The board is the single most powerful group representing the shareholders of the company. No other individual or group is empowered to and accountable for governance, although there are many players contributing to some aspect of directing and controlling the company.

A best practice is to elect board members each year, although some companies have a multi-year cycle wherein some board members retire at end of each cycle, but may be eligible for reelection. The slate of board members for election by shareholders is prepared by the governance committee of the board. Each director and collectively, the board and its committees are charged with the responsibility to direct and control the management with a view to maximize shareholder long-term interests and to comply with laws and regulations applicable to the company. Chapter 6 explores board structure and function; Chapter 10 examines the board in action.

Management

An incorporated company has existence separate from its owners and is responsible for all its actions and omissions. But it is an incorporeal entity and, therefore, cannot act by itself. The destiny of the company is shaped by its leaders, the senior executives. Since management makes decisions and acts upon them on behalf of the company, management represents the company. The result is that the board's efforts to govern are directed toward senior management as agents of the company.

Because of the separation of risk takers (shareholders) from the company, proper governance begins with adequate and timely disclosure by the management. Any information that is believed to have a material impact on the shareholder's decision to continue to remain invested in the company is required to be communicated in a timely and transparent manner. The interaction between the board and management is discussed in Chapter 11.

Whereas there could be countless executives in a large, global corporation, in corporate governance, we typically think of a select number of top executives, primarily the CEO and the CFO. This group is sometimes described as senior management. Although shareholders exercise influence through their communication with the board, including proxy votes, they also receive information from, and are engaged with senior management. Conference calls hosted by the CEO and the CFO are an example of communication between management and shareholders. Shareholder communication and engagement is discussed in Chapter 12.

GOVERNMENT AND THE REGULATORS

In addition to laws of the state in which a company is incorporated, the federal laws and regulations apply to the conduct of the company. The government has an interest in ensuring that the financial markets are stable and the flow of investment is guided by efficient markets that facilitate absorption of relevant information in the stock price as soon as the information is made public. In the securities market, the primary agency that represents the federal government is the Securities and Exchange Commission (SEC).

The availability of financial information that is fairly stated and is reliable is central to an investor's decision to buy, sell, or hold their investment in the company. As independent and objective professionals, external auditors (also called public accountants) conduct an audit (a review) of financial statements annually (quarterly) and provide an opinion regarding the veracity of the financial numbers. Until the enactment of the Sarbanes Oxley Act (SOX), independent auditors were self-regulated by their professional organization, the AICPA. The SOX requires that the auditors conducting an independent audit of public companies will be regulated by a newly created non-profit organization, the PCAOB. This body regulates the public company auditors and also sets auditing standards.

Although not directly involved as a regulator, the Financial Accounting Standards Board (FASB) impacts the accounting principles public companies must follow in preparing their financial information. Ultimately, the SEC is responsible for endorsing the accounting standards promulgated by the FASB.

The trio – SEC, PCAOB, and FASB – represent a powerful ecosystem impacting governance of companies. The latter two categorically influence the nature and quality of financial information about public companies accessible to the investors.

SEC, PCAOB, and FASB

The U.S. Congress is responsible at the federal level for laws that affect corporate governance. In turn, Congress has designated the SEC to oversee governance regulation and enforce the securities laws (e.g., the Sarbanes Oxley Act).

While the laws as such cannot be role players in the same sense as shareholders, managers, and board members are, it should be noted that the governing state and federal laws set the threshold of legal compliance by management on behalf of the company. Backed by the law, regulatory agencies such as the SEC provide the "common law" applicable to publicly traded companies. In the USA, the incorporation of a company occurs at the state level, so the laws of the state in which the company is incorporated trigger compliance. The state of Delaware is the most popular state for incorporation of companies, for it is at the forefront of corporate governance regulation. In addition to laws of the state in which the company is incorporated, federal statutes have become increasingly important as the intervention of the federal government in Corporate America has gained foothold. For example, the Sarbanes Oxley Act and the Dodd-Frank Act have introduced numerous additional requirements that corporations have to meet regardless of the state in which they are incorporated. Undoubtedly, the public company responsibility for compliance has greatly increased over time.

Since shareholders are at the center of corporate capital formation, it is expected that the securities law would focus on defining regulatory requirements with the shareholder in mind. For all securities-related enforcement, the single most important federal government agency accountable is the Securities and Exchange Commission (SEC). The SEC has an overarching goal of facilitating capital formation to sustain economic growth. Besides this economy-wide goal, it also serves as a guardian of investors; that is, it protects investors and ensures maintenance of law and order in capital markets operations. The SEC is organized into five major divisions: corporation finance (oversees corporate disclosure of information to the investors); trading and markets (exercises duty to maintain fair, orderly and efficient markets); investment management (manages investor protection and promotes capital formation); enforcement (recommends and carries out civil enforcement actions and works with enforcement agencies to file criminal cases where deemed necessary); and economic and risk analysis (assists rulemaking and policy development and provides risk-related insights to support SEC functions).

To ensure shareholder influence, disclosure of all relevant information is necessary and should have the regulatory force behind it. Thus, it is mandated that investors have access to relevant information about a security prior to making an investment decision. Moreover, since financial markets and stock exchanges are served by intermediaries such as broker/dealers, advisors, funds and rating agencies, those engaged in securities trading must put investors' interests first. The SEC provides oversight on these activities to maintain fairness and honesty and discourage misrepresentation and fraud. The presence of financial reporting fraud in all areas of corporate existence prompted lawmakers to enact and enforce regulations that would minimize the occurrence of fraud.

In the aftermath of Enron and WorldCom meltdowns and the audit firm Arthur Andersen's demise, lawmakers introduced through the SOX new provisions concerning disclosure and communication of financial information and the auditing of company books. This was the first major overhaul of the Securities Act of 1943. It appears that the primary motivation behind these provisions was the thinking that audit quality is slipping. Therefore, the SOX introduced an independent non-profit organization, Public Company Accounting Oversight Board (PCAOB). PCAOB, under the supervision of the SEC, operates more like the auditor's auditor, enacting the auditing standards for public company audits and inspecting the audit work done by independent auditors.

Financial Accounting Standards Board (FASB)

Because much of substantive company information communicated to shareholders is financial in nature, it is important to recognize the FASB and its role. An independent non-profit organization, the FASB sets accounting standards using due process, interprets and illustrates how these standards apply to business, and facilitates any other questions or queries regarding the accounting standards.

The FASB works closely with professional accounting bodies in the U.S.A., primarily the American Institute of Certified Public Accountants (AICPA). The AICPA provides certification of accounting and auditing professionals and regulates its members. License to practice as a public accountant is issued by the state boards of public accountancy organized in each state. The four largest public accounting firms fill the role of an independent (or external) auditor in nearly half of the very large public companies. These are Deloitte, PricewaterhouseCoopers (PWC), Ernst & Young (EY), and KPMG, collectively called the Big Four. The AICPA is actively engaged in the proceedings of the FASB.

The financial accounting standards set by the FASB are applicable to companies incorporated in the U.S.A. and to foreign companies whose shares or American Depository Receipts (ADRs) are traded on the U.S. stock exchanges. Other public companies globally may choose other accounting standards, depending on the jurisdiction of applicable laws and conventions. Among the widely used accounting standards internationally are those promulgated by the International Accounting Standards Board (IASB). Broadly, international accounting standards are principles-based, while the U.S. accounting standards by FASB are more detailed, rules-based.

COREGULATORS, FACILITATORS, AND CONSULTANTS

This group of individuals or entities is generally described as assisting those in charge of governance with their actions which contribute to the governance process. For example, independent auditors provide an opinion on the financial statements of a public company whose books they audit; they also are required to pursue any signs of financial fraud. The efforts of independent auditors help ensure that the financial information shared by the company with investors is fairly represented and is prepared in accordance with the GAAP. Because coregulators, facilitators, and consultants participate in some way in the governance process, they are subject to the same requirements as the independent directors, such as independence, objectivity, competency in the field of work, and absence of conflict of interest.

Coregulators

Coregulators are those elements in the governance ecosystem that participate in their unique role in corporate governance. Thus, part of the burden of converging on effective regulation of a company falls on coregulators. Coregulators are not consultants, collaborators, or facilitators; they are presumed to be actively involved in the governance process. Because they are coregulators, some of the primary requirements imposed upon independent directors also carry over to coregulators. For example, coregulators should be independent and have no conflict of interests and should not enter in related party transactions with the company they help regulate.

Two major groups of coregulators are the internal audit function (IAF) and external (independent) auditors. Internal auditors are a part of the management and, as a result, not entirely independent. Their domain is two-fold. First, they are consultants to management, assisting in guiding process owners in risk management, improving efficiency, and creating value. In this capacity, internal auditors are allies of management with full responsibility to actively collaborate with others in the organization. In this role, internal auditors are not independent. Second, they are internal "watchdogs," independently testing internal controls to identify significant deficiencies or material weaknesses, if any. Internal auditors should brief management on their findings and suggest changes to improve the control framework. They also help detect employee and management fraud. This part of their work may be relied upon by the external auditors in their review of internal controls. Therefore, it is critical that in this role, internal auditors are independent in their judgments. For example, those auditors who recommended certain controls should not be asked to verify if those controls exist and are working effectively. Lack of independence would cause the external auditors to not rely on the findings of the IAF; instead, they may repeat controls testing and this, at a minimum, would increase audit costs. Also, it may have an impact on the corporate image in terms of regard for independent functioning of the internal audit, especially with respect to risk management and controls testing.

These two spheres of internal auditing also are important for the board of directors in assessing how well management is balancing the two domains of the internal audit function. Too much stress on the consulting dimension would simply mean less time to do controls testing and evaluation, and this may be considered as a "red flag." The board should discuss with management the overall split of resource allocation between the two major spheres of internal auditing. Chapter 8 discusses in detail the role of IAF.

External, independent auditors represent a formidable coregulator. They are required to be independent professionals, competent in their role as auditors of financial statements. They should exercise due care; where they suspect any fraud, manipulation, or misrepresentation of financial information, they should pursue the trail until a final determination is reached whether the evidence points to an act of fraud. As independent examiners of the company's books, it is important that while they work with management, they should report to the audit committee of the board of directors. Chapter 9 discusses in detail the role of external auditors.

Facilitators and Consultants

Even though the board members individually and collectively may have considerable expertise in various fields relevant in the exercise of their duty, it is quite likely that they do not have depth in everything they need to direct and control the company. As a result, the board may retain consultants in various fields as and when it deems necessary to do so. For example, to set the compensation plan for its executives, the board may retain compensation experts to assist them with information and insights otherwise inaccessible to the board. Similarly, experts in securities, securities regulation, cybersecurity, and other fields may be recruited by the board to address questions, find answers, and generally help steer the company through unique or difficult times.

Advisory groups, such as the Institutional Shareholder Services (ISS) and Glass Lewis & Co., provide corporate governance solutions and services. For example, they help the board navigate through a class-action suit or assist in addressing concerns brought up by the SEC regarding governance of the company; they also offer routine services, such as end-to-end support for managing proxies. Because such advice could result in significant influence over shareholders and how they vote, the SEC has been planning to provide new guidelines for proxy advisors. The aim is to produce greater transparency into how proxy advisors make recommendations on director elections and other ballots placed before the shareholders. It is believed that proxy advisors should disclose conflict of interest, if any, in their relationship with client companies.

Compared to the advisory groups, OECD and NACD are non-profit institutions with a different mission. Organizations like OECD offer advice regarding broad policy matters while NACD engages specifically in board matters, issues, and solutions as well as education of board members. Collectively, advisory groups – both for-profit and non-profit – help identify issues and offer advice on how to address them.

STOCK EXCHANGES

Stock exchanges play a dual role. First, they facilitate transactions (buy, sell, etc.) in securities of a company listed on the stock exchange. This allows investors to freely exercise their right to own shares or divest them easily. The investors may use any and all information, including information disseminated by the company, to make the decision to invest or divest. Without the mobility of funds invested, the separation of ownership from management is unsustainable.

Second, the stock exchange "lists" the company stock for trading on the exchange. The company should apply for listing. The exchange exercises due diligence prior to approving the listing; upon approval, the securities of the company may be traded by any investor. At the time of initial listing, the company must meet the requirements of the stock exchange. For example, NASDAQ requires an initial bid price per share of $4. Only listed companies' securities may be traded on the stock exchange; securities of companies not listed on any stock exchange may be traded as over-the-counter transactions on a dealer network, not a centralized exchange. To keep the listing active, the company must meet the requirements set by the stock exchange for continued listing. These requirements boost the company governance and are usually in harmony with agencies that regulate securities markets, such as the SEC. A company in default could present a plan to the stock exchange concerning how it plans to return to full compliance of the requirements.

In essence, the U.S. stock exchanges as part of the capital markets are regulated by the SEC. There are many stock exchanges worldwide. As related to Corporate America, two are quite prominent: NYSE (New York Stock Exchange) Euronext and NASDAQ, which is an American multinational financial services corporation that owns and operates the NASDAQ stock market and eight European stock exchanges. The NYSE lists large corporations in various sectors while technology intensive firms are dominant among the companies listed on NASDAQ.

Actions of dealer-traders, rating agencies (e.g. Morningstar), fund managers, and investment advisors impact shareholders and the company equity valuations. As a result, the all-embracing governance rules also cover the requirements that guide proper, fair, and transparent behavior of those facilitating investment decisions and transactions in the stock market. This group only tangentially impacts the governance at the company level; however, it has significant obligations toward investors and the overall conduct in the market.

MAKING SENSE OF GOVERNANCE

To understand what governance is and how it is accomplished, we need to grasp the nature of role players, what they do, and how they contribute to the governance process. Moreover, it is important to know the role of each participant, whether it is a governed entity, the governor, or the facilitator. In the chain of principal-agent relationship, each role may signify the presence of a principal, or an agent. This is important to consider because the fiduciary duty flows from the agent to the principal. The rights and duties of each role must be clarified to comprehend the dynamics involved in the governance process. Not only the individual role player's impact, but also how it converges into a larger picture of governance should be considered. It is also essential to know how they interact with each other and thus exert influence on the outcomes of the governance process.

BIBLIOGRAPHY

de Kluyver, C. A. 2013. *A Primer on Corporate Governance*, Second Edition. New York: Business Expert Press.

Monks, R. A. G. and Minow, L. 2012. *Corporate Governance*, Fifth Edition. New York: John Wiley & Sons.

Podkul, C. 2019. Proxy advisor sues SEC over new rules. *The Wall Street Journal*, November 2–3, B11.

Pratt, J. 2013. *Financial Accounting in an Economic Context*, Ninth Edition. New York: John Wiley & Sons.

CHAPTER 6

The Board of Directors

The board of directors can be described as the hub of governance activity. It is where the "buck stops"; that is, the accountability of the board is unquestionable and final. Almost all other role players in the governance space are directly or indirectly connected with the board. As the designee of the company's shareholders, it "calls the shots" on every aspect of governance, keeping management in check. The board-management relationship is not adversarial; however, the final call on how things should be done is made by the board. This is not so much on day-to-day activities, but rather with respect to performance, planning, compliance, and culture of the company.

THE BOARD AS A GOVERNING BODY

In a public company setting, the board of directors is the single, most powerful body responsible for the governance of the company on behalf of its stakeholders, primarily the shareholders. Organizationally, the board sits between management and the shareholders. The board is the agent of its principal, the shareholders; protection of their interests is the primary duty of the board. On the other side, the board is the principal in relation to its agent, management. Thus, on behalf of the shareholders, the board is charged with the oversight of management's actions and performance. As representatives of the company's shareholders, board members are elected by shareholders for a designated term; often, the election is for just one year; continuation beyond that year may be subject to reelection for the following year. Where the term is longer than one year, a group of directors exits the board on a multi-year cycle; a purpose in defining terms longer than one year is to not lose the experience and wisdom of the collective body all at one time!

In corporate governance, a clear distinction is made between those board members who qualify as independent and those who don't. Normally, the board consists of a mix of independent and non-independent directors, where the majority should be comprised of independent directors. Former employees of the company, such as the past CEO, may qualify as non-independent, non-executive affiliate members of the board if they exited the company within the past three years. Such affiliate members potentially contribute value through their past experience with the company. They are not independent, but their degree of independence may be higher than that of a non-independent director. A non-executive director, or outside director, is considered independent if the director meets the legal requirements of independence. All outside directors who fail to meet the tests of independence are considered non-independent. For example, a board member who represents a particular interest group, such as a hedge fund that has invested substantially in the company, is considered a non-independent director, presumably because the director represents a select segment of the owners and may focus mainly on serving only their interests.

Since the board constantly interacts with management, it is imperative that some degree of overlap between the board and management should prove helpful. This question is automatically addressed where the board chair is also the CEO of the company. In other cases, some of the executives – typically the CEO and perhaps the CFO – may be elected to the board. Without the management representation on the board, "one hand would not know what the other is doing." In the absence of such overlap, coordination and the amount of communication between the board and management would increase substantially and the trust between the two may need to be nurtured in some other way. Because they represent management, executive directors are considered non-independent.

While a majority of directors must qualify as legally independent, the role of non-independent directors should not be marginalized. They have a special role to play; each non-independent director may bring to the board expertise and skills that are much needed to create long-term value for the shareholder. In fact, the European Union – especially Germany – recognizes in its governance requirements a separate board, called the management board, comprised of representatives of labor and outside experts (legal counsel, security consultants, etc.) who may not qualify as independent. The role of the management board is discussed in Table 6.1.

TABLE 6.1 Role of management boards

A one-tier board, the only board of directors of the company, is a norm in the United States and, generally, in North America. However, some of the EU member states, Japan, and other regions of the world have adopted the practice of having two-tier boards instead of a unitary board, where the top-tier board is recognized as the supervisory board; the additional group is separately identified as the management board. The primary responsibility for representing the shareholders still rests with the supervisory board, which oversees the management board.

The reason for having a second-tier management board is that while those who provide capital deserve a voice, it is essential that labor as a factor of production also is offered an avenue to voice its concerns and provide input. For example, if the company is considering dropping a major product line or permanently shutting down a plant with a significant number of employees, representatives of employees serving on the management board would be concerned about the job losses, how those laid off would be compensated, the re-training of outgoing employees, and assisting them in seeking another job. Broadly, the management board is responsible to exercise oversight on the operations and transactions of the company.

The management board is comprised of managers and other employees of the company, and may include outsiders. There usually is no overlap of members between the two boards, although the two boards likely communicate with each other regularly.

Management boards have a duty to inform the supervisory board on issues and challenges faced by the company and offer advice on how to deal with them. While such input from the management is advisory only, the supervisory board is likely to give it serious consideration in its deliberations. Any resolutions passed by the management board require approval of the supervisory board. Practically, having a management board potentially permits the company leadership to move closer to stakeholder perspective, for other stakeholders get a voice through the management board.

In unitary board structures, the board can seek advice of appropriate experts, including employees and outside consultants, as and when the board deems necessary. However, this is ad hoc and the board has to determine the need each time. If an issue warrants a sustained consideration for some time, the board may appoint a committee to serve in a distinct capacity.

(*Continued*)

TABLE 6.1 (Cont.)

It is likely that a two-tier board structure creates more governance challenges. Differences in opinions and perspectives on various issues facing the company are likely to arise between the two boards, and conflict resolution in such cases may be warranted. Some of the differences may arise because of the contrast in risk tolerance of each board. The supervisory board's decision is final; however, some degree of communication between the two boards would be necessary to explain the final decision to the management board. The potential benefits of a two-tier structure will be lost if mutual trust and respect is not maintained between the two boards.

THE BOARD FUNCTION

Any public company's board basically devotes time to two major areas: strategy and policy; and monitoring and compliance. The Cadbury report (1992) emphasized that governance is about performance and conformance. Without conformance to regulations and the law, the company would suffer from regulatory investigations and likely would get distracted, and may even experience reputational loss, causing further economic deterioration of the company. Perhaps as a result of this, corporate boards typically devote a great deal of time to conformance, even if it is at the sacrifice of adequate performance oversight.

A board member's accountability is not so much in terms of the outcome as the process followed. Broadly, one could describe a board member's commitment as having to do "the right thing," although this may not fully result in doing "the thing right." Moreover, there are other ways to look at the board duties. According to one view, the board has two overarching mandates: the mandate to advise and the mandate to oversee. Blanketing the two mandates is the legal duty of directors generally described as the triad of fiduciary duties: due care, good faith, and loyalty. Due care implies that the director acted on an informed basis, with care any prudent person would take under similar circumstances. Diligence and due care require an active attempt to understand the issue while making inquiries warranted based on the director's background. For example, a director who is also a lawyer should pursue the analysis from the legal angle, and a director who has an accounting background should also solicit and shift through relevant evidence from the accounting perspective. In essence, due care means best efforts to question the issues before making judgment.

Good faith represents honesty, conscientiousness, and fairness in the discharge of one's responsibilities as a director, with a view to act in the best interests of *all* stakeholders, particularly the shareholders. The exercise of good faith would prohibit the tendencies to cheat or delay the communication of relevant information, to falsify information, and to take advantage of the position of privilege as a director. To avoid open discussion and instead "fall in line" with the rest of the board members would probably signal breach of good faith, for such behavior would implicate the loss of shareholder voice.

The duty of loyalty suggests that the director acted in an honest belief that the action taken was in the best interests of the company. Putting one's own interests ahead of the company's interest would mean a compromise of loyalty. Actions that would potentially yield personal gains at the expense of the company's benefit would mean that the director has breached loyalty.

While each case is different in terms of the board involvement as the guardian of shareholder interests, there are some clearly identifiable functional areas that are common to all public company boards: (1) recruit senior management, especially the CEO; (2) approve corporate vision and strategic plan; (3) set the tone-from-the-top; and (4) determine risk appetite. The CEO is the driver of the corporate engine; practically, the CEO is visualized as the most influential image of the company, the so-called persona of the corporeal entity. A poor choice of the CEO would indicate that the vision of the company may not be achieved as well as hoped. Therefore, recruiting for this top position is a critical task of the board; the choice of a CEO would reverberate throughout the tenure of the chief executive through his decisions and conduct. Firing a CEO that didn't work out and hiring a replacement may sound easy, but it would take considerable energy to implement it. Meanwhile, the damage done by the poor choice sets the company behind in its mission.

The tone from the top is set by the board and senior management. While this may be a soft area, creating the right tone and culture within the company is very important, for it lays down the bar for employee behavior at all levels. What the leadership does not emphasize, not just in words but in deeds as well, will be ignored and treated as unimportant. Once in place, tone from the top needs continuous nurturing; it requires careful monitoring to ensure that the tone remains strong, and there are no cracks showing up. An occasional audit of the tone by experts in the field could help as well.

The spirit of the corporation mirrors in its vision. Therefore, the board should strive to build a vision for the company. Sourced in the company's vision is the strategic plan, a course charted for the company's journey over time. The board's impetus in shaping the company's strategic plan is essential. Finally, the determination of risk appetite that is aligned with shareholders' expectations is an important step for the board. It is only fitting that the company should not take any more risk than its investors would want, although this may not be easy to determine.

COMPOSITION OF THE BOARD

The board size varies across public companies. There is no requirement to have a specific number of directors on the board. Companies with annual revenues of less than a billion dollars often have a small board (about five members) and larger companies may choose to have several more. A majority of the members have to be independent, that is, should meet the criteria set for qualifying as an independent director. Only those who qualify as independent can serve on certain board committees.

As discussed earlier, management representation on the board is highly likely. If the chairman of the board (discussed next) is also the CEO of the company, the board may decide not to have another executive of the company serve on the company board. If the chairman and CEO roles are separated, the CEO is likely to be elected to the board. Other executives, such as the CFO or in-house legal counsel, may also serve on the board. Non-executive directors from outside may be selected based on the needs of the board. For example, the board may need someone with background in law and compliance, strategy formulation, or technology relevant to the company. Or it may be that the board is looking for someone with a solid network in the company's industry space; the difficulty might be that an ideal candidate is already serving on multiple boards and does not have time or interest in joining yet another board. Finally, hedge funds with substantial investment in voting shares of the company may dictate appointment of their representative on the board. In the end, the goal should be to bring together people of high integrity, transparency, and candor who can work as a cohesive force in the interest of the shareholders.

Chairman of the Board

As a designated leader of the board of directors, the chairman has sweeping influence over the company's destiny. The chair could play a major hand in setting the tone at the top, establishing strategic direction of the company, and shaping the overall corporate climate which provides signals to employees and managers in terms of what is exceptional, acceptable, or outright wrong and will not be tolerated. The chair works closely with directors and frequently with the CEO. The chair most likely understands well the company's risks, business model, operations, and strategy.

Among the duties of the chairman are to recruit board members, recruit the CEO and help recruit other senior managers, require a succession plan for key managers, guide and where necessary, help the senior management, ensure that the code of conduct is established, understand the risk appetite of the company, and engage with the shareholders. While this is not a fulltime job, it essentially entails nearly complete submersion in the affairs of the company; being available to direct and control the company and its management in coordination with the board is the bottom line.

This outsize role requires that the person has leadership characteristics. Ethical behavior, a broad understanding of laws and regulations pertinent to the company, effective communication, thinking on the feet, and understanding human motivation are among myriad attributes that a chair should possess. Above all, the chair's ability to work "in sync" with the senior management is probably the most important litmus test of a successful chair.

Lead Independent Director

Under certain circumstances, the chairman of the board may not qualify as an independent director. For example, when the chair and CEO roles are combined, the executive director is not independent. When this condition occurs, the influence of the independent directors on the board is under an aura of the non-independent person leading the board. To limit the influence of the chair in such cases, the independent directors are asked to appoint their leader, called lead independent director. The

TABLE 6.2 Separation of Board Chair and CEO roles – issues and challenges

One of the hotly debated issues in corporate governance is the separation of the chairman of the board from the CEO role in the same company. Although highly recommended as best practice, it is not a legal requirement for public companies. Sometimes, the SEC has intervened to force the separation of the two roles, as in the case of Tesla in 2019. The reasons in favor of and against the separation are many and often valid. Where the chairman is also the founder of the board who had the vision to launch the business, emotional attachment with the company may result in resistance against the separation, even when the founder has run out of energy and ideas. On the flip side, who could be a more passionate leader than the one who crafted the mission? Does this mean, however, that the two roles need to be combined into one to provide unchecked power in the hands of one person? Adding to this dilemma is the chairman's control over the voting shares in the company, allowing them to accept or reject almost anything because of a majority voice. Perhaps this is appropriate, for as an investor, the chair would lose, or gain, the most; the risk belongs to the person and therefore, influence accorded is in line with the ownership. At a minimum, this illustrates why the issue of separation of board chair from the CEO is contentious.

Depending on the specific situation, separating the two roles may be a good trade-off in specific circumstances. For example, as discussed in Chapter 13, if the person holding both roles is highly self-regarding, it may help prevent or detect financial fraud provided the two roles are separated. Where the two roles remain combined, it is necessary for the board to periodically discuss in an executive session whether it is time to split the two roles.

Where the joint appointment continues, it is necessary for the independent directors to elect a lead independent director. The lead director has the authority to call executive sessions, approve the board agenda, represent the chairman in his absence, ensure that issues that came up in executive sessions are followed up, and be available for communication with shareholders.

combined Chair-CEO role merges two powerful positions into one, creating higher probability of a compromise of checks and balances. The separation of board chair and the CEO role is discussed in Table 6.2.

SUBCOMMITTEES OF THE BOARD

Depending on its needs, the board may form several subgroups or committees with a specific charge. Ongoing committees of the board are also called standing committees. A minimum of three standing committees is a requirement: the audit committee, the compensation committee, and the governance committee. The company should adopt a formal written charter for at least the audit and compensation committee; the charter should specify the scope of committees' responsibilities and the means by which it carries out those responsibilities. Rights and responsibilities of the committee articulated in the charter empower the committee to meet its obligations.

Audit Committee

The audit committee, also called the audit and compliance committee, is responsible for oversight on financial accounting and reporting processes of the company, internal controls over financial accounting and reporting, and regulatory compliance related to financial matters. The audit committee is also accountable for audits of the company's financial statements by an independent public accounting firm registered with the PCAOB. In this regard, it is responsible for approving, or recommending the board for approval, the appointment, compensation, and retention of the company's external auditors. For internal and external auditors, the committee functions as the primary group for engagement with the board. The minimum number of directors on the committee should be three, all of whom must qualify as independent. If the board does not have an audit committee, the entire board is responsible for these duties.

Compensation Committee

The compensation committee is responsible for setting current and long-term compensation for key executives, and to exercise oversight on compensation issues and succession planning.

Governance Committee

Also called governance and nominating committee, the governance committee's charge is to recommend candidates for election as directors; nominate members of the standing committees of the board; approve change in size of the board; recruit new board members; conduct evaluations of the directors, the board as a whole, and its committees; and periodically review proposed changes to the company's governance documents.

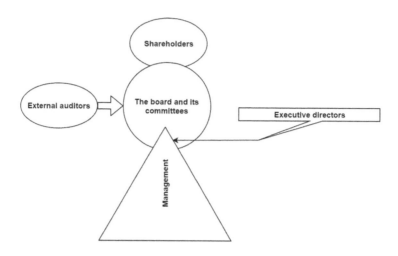

FIGURE 6.1   The board and its relationships.

Figure 6.1 shows an overview of the board and its relationships with shareholders and the management.

DIRECTOR QUALIFICATIONS

A fundamental obligation of a director is reflected in the business judgment rule (or presumption), which signifies that a court will uphold the decisions of a director as long as they are made in good faith, with care that a reasonably prudent person would use, and with the reasonable belief that the director is acting in the best interests of the corporation. While this is a broad baseline requirement, the bar these days is quite high. Most director candidates are educated, experienced, well-versed in general legal and regulatory challenges, and savvy in their communication skills. They may or may not have substantial expertise in the industry to which the company belongs, or significant depth – at least initially – in the business model and operations of the company seeking the candidacy for the board appointment. Besides, not all directors are effective in every aspect of the business; some may be expert in strategic planning, while someone else could provide insights on tax planning or business processes. For any questions that arise before the board, the board has the discretion to engage an expert in the field. This would permit the board to seek advice from outside the board as and when necessary.

Five essential qualities of an effective board member include being dedicated and committed, able to lead and influence others, straightforward and impartial, knowledgeable and an insatiable learner, values discretion and confidentiality. However, what is most needed in a director is candor. Without candor, transparency would probably be less helpful. As a group, the board could suffer from groupthink, as if the entire board consists of only one member! Diversity of opinion, debates on issues with a view to find good answers, and eloquent articulation of issues – these are of great value to the board.

Director Independence

Only a high level of integrity in a person would nearly guarantee an independent voice of the person, regardless of how connected the person might be to the company and its affiliates. As discussed in Chapter 13, a person's disposition is a close indicator of the person's moral identity; high moral identity is likely to result in greater independence and thus, a righteous behavior to protect shareholder interests. However, integrity is hard to measure and monitor, so the legal recourse is to find surrogates that would provide reasonable assurance of lack of self-interest in the company. Typical measures used to assess director independence are: (1) the director or his family, including extended family, has no involvement in the company, including its affiliates, subsidiaries, or collaborators; (2) no relation of the director is employed by the company or its affiliates, subsidiaries or collaborators; and (3) no beneficial contractual relationship exists with the company.

The attributes of independence are summarized in Table 6.3 and diagramed in Figure 6.2. Independence is a state of mind. In corporate governance, independence is construed as assurance of fearlessness, courage, and fortitude to exercise one's duty as a director. It can also be described as the director having the "guts" to do the right thing even if it materializes in disagreement with the powerful management representatives. Independence is not a panacea, only a prerequisite; to quote Warren Buffett from his 2002 letter to shareholders of Berkshire Hathaway, the independent director must also be "business-savvy, interested, and shareholder oriented."

TABLE 6.3 Attributes of independence

Ideally, it would be best to mandate independence in fact. However, this is difficult to measure and therefore, not enforceable. If anything, it may result in inconsistent application of the norm of independence. Therefore, the regulatory requirements focus on the measurement of independence in appearance with the hope that this will come close to independence in fact.

In practice, it is clear that non-material instances should be ignored in testing if independence in appearance exists. Also, time expired since the past relationship potentially jeopardizing independence is an important consideration. A CEO who left the company ten years ago is probably less conflicted than a CEO who departed last year.

The application of various tests of independence is targeted to both the self and his or her relations. The notion behind this is that one may be in a conflicted relationship because one's relative is involved in the relationship and thus, in essence, the beneficial relationship that compromises independence exists.

There are four tests applied to determine if a person in the present or prospective role of a director is independent. Each test is applied to both the director and his or her relations. Leaving out the specifics, these are described below in general terms:

Benefit test: Outside of the director compensation, the person is not receiving any other emoluments directly or indirectly.

Past relationship test: To be independent, one needs to not have any connection with the company for a reasonable period of time.

Coregulator test: The director shall not have any affiliation with those who help regulate the company by providing appropriate services. For example, the external auditors provide an opinion on the fairness of financial statements. Hence, an independent director or his or her relation should not be employed, or otherwise render services to the auditor. The independent role of coregulators may be compromised in this manner.

Interlocking test: Corporations A and B have an interlocking condition if a director or executive of A is also a director of B. An interlocking condition may be indirect, where a director of each of A and B sit on the board of Corporation C. Interlocks may help establish solid business relationships across companies; however, the independence of directors involved may be compromised.

The sources that compromise such independence are identified by assessing what other relationships with the company where the individual serves as a director could come in the way of thinking of best interests of the shareholders. The degree of independence may change as the circumstances impacting self-interest in the company change. Where there is even a hint of possible conflict of interest and thus

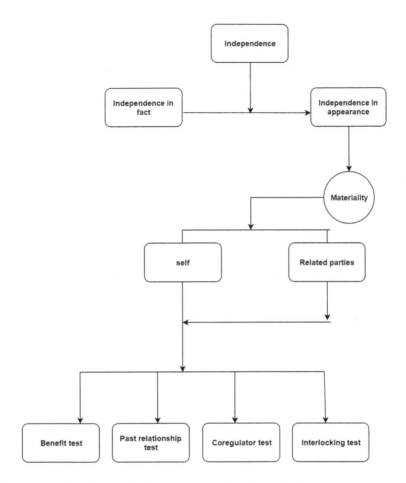

FIGURE 6.2   Attributes of independence – A schematic view.

potential loss of independence, the director should recuse from the discussion and resolution of question or decision under consideration. For example, where the company is negotiating a contract with another company in which the director has interest, it is only appropriate for the director to not influence the outcome. As Warren Buffett, the CEO and Chair of Berkshire Hathaway puts it, Berkshire doesn't allow any conflict of interest transactions or relationships unless the company clearly benefits from it; otherwise, it would be best to just avoid creating the conflict.

Conflict of interest issues are not just for the board or management; they arise for everyone, especially persons occupying positions of influence. In 2019 the mayor of the city of Baltimore, Ms. Catherine Pugh, stepped down from her position, for she had resorted to, or passively endorsed, the exploitation of her influence as a leader. While she was on the board of directors at the University of Maryland Medical System, she was paid by the institution $500,000 for 100,000 copies of her children's book, *Healthy Holly*. During her tenure as mayor, insurers and a financial-services firm purchased numerous copies of the book, hoping to gain preferential treatment from the mayor. While not all of this may be Ms. Pugh's doing – she cannot control who buys her books – the lesson is to stay clear of any and all kinds of potential conflicts, perceived or actual. To repair the damage, the least Ms. Pugh could have done was to return, where possible, the amount of royalty she earned from the book sales to the purchaser.

The most visible conflict of interest is when the chairman of the board also serves as the CEO. As discussed previously, this may not be the best practice, but it is permitted in the USA, provided the proxy statement includes an explanation of why the two roles are combined into one. This particular conflict of interest is somewhat alleviated by the board choosing to have a lead independent director who is supposed to provide counterbalance on possible negative consequences of the combined role.

Can a conflict-free board as a decision-making unit deliver superior decision-making? Not necessarily. One study found that while diversity in the board may be a good thing to have, increased diversity results in superior decision-making only when (1) the board is free from conflict *and* (2) acts as a cohesive group. The cohesiveness may be suboptimal when directors align and separate across board members with their diverse attributes (e.g., length of tenure, share ownership, insider or independent, gender), thus forming "fault-lines," which may negatively impact group dynamics (e.g., increasing friction, hampering decision-making processes, reducing information exchange between directors).

Total independence cannot always be assured, for it is a state of mind which could change over time. Moreover, independence, even when present in large measure, does not imply soundness of judgment. Since conflict of interest cannot be completely avoided in most cases, appropriate governance measures should be encouraged. At times, such measures are in the form of best practice; however, some measures may be required as part of the compliance regime. For example, where board chair and the CEO roles are combined, the best practice is for the independent directors to elect a lead independent director to fill the vacuum created by the board chair representing both the board and management. To monitor other conflicts of interest situations, a regulatory requirement is to report related-party transactions in the annual report (SEC, Form 10k).

Director Appointment and Tenure

The board's governance committee typically recommends candidates to fill vacancies that arise over time, due to resignation, death, or some other circumstances. Sometimes, if appropriate, the board may vote to not fill the vacancy and instead, reduce the board size permanently. In appointing a new board member, the board votes on the nominating committee's recommendation. The newly appointed director may choose to run for election by shareholders at the next annual meeting of the company.

Once the slate of board members is complete, there may not be room for change in the board membership unless someone with influential ownership of voting shares chooses to initiate a change. The evidence suggests that board members serve for a long time, often in excess of ten years. With such long tenure, there may not be any room for new entrants and this could be a mixed blessing.

One way to introduce new board members is to increase the board size. However, the board size typically remains constant; only the board, when it deems necessary, may vote to increase or decrease the size. The need for change in the board composition may arise from forces such as activist shareholders or changes in the regulatory requirements. For example, the Sarbanes-Oxley Act imposed a new requirement that at least one member of the audit committee, but not necessarily the committee chair, should be financially literate, that is, should meet the requirements of the audit committee financial expertise. As a result, boards that lacked such expertise opted to add a qualified person to the board.

The recruitment of a board member is an intentional exercise on the part of the board. A clear articulation of the strengths of the current board is necessary and, as well, a thoughtful statement of what the board is looking for in the recruit is necessary. Without this, the gap in the board's collective competencies and skills will not be bridged and at the same time, redundancies might occur. As an example of how a board effectively recruits for a new board member, consider this. A public company in the business of IT outsourcing grew significantly over time. Its data centers in India employed thousands of IT-skilled people to serve the needs of customers worldwide and primarily in the USA. The company had to comply with regulatory requirements in India as well as in the USA, where it was incorporated. As a result, the board opened a search for a new director with certain qualifications: understanding of cultures of both countries, knowledge of financial accounting and reporting standards, regulatory requirements and taxation in both countries, and ability to work across cultures. This illustrates the fact that board seats are meant to serve the fiduciary responsibilities as agents of the shareholders, and in the process of recruiting, the board may seek additional expertise missing in the board. As discussed in Chapter 3, the board of Boeing corporation has added safety-related experience as a criterion for recruitment of future directors. This consideration surfaced only after the 737 MAX disaster; however, it is now a prerequisite for future candidates for directorship at Boeing.

One reason for changes in the board membership could be an active and aggressive expression of dissatisfaction by influential shareholders, including hedge funds, with the performance of the board in exercising appropriate oversight to advance shareholder interests. For example, an activist hedge fund, Barrington Capital Group LP, asserted that L. Brands' board members lacked the independence or skills needed to navigate drastic changes in the lingerie market. As a result, the company – through its board – agreed that it would replace some directors at the next annual meeting with a view to increase board diversity. Similarly, in a proxy battle with a group of activist investors dissatisfied with the company performance, Bed Bath & Beyond replaced five independent directors and caused the company cofounder to step down.

Director Motivation and Compensation

There are significant challenges facing a director. Directors could be sued by shareholder(s) for nonperformance of their duties, or they could be liable for not exercising good judgment. Moreover, the usual demands placed on the director's availability and commitment of time is not immaterial. Even for a relatively small and growing company with revenues in the range of $500 million, the task of the board could be quite challenging and time consuming, and could take in excess of 500 hours annually in self-study, meeting attendance in person and online, travel, and networking.

An important consideration for director candidates is the availability of time in light of the candidate's current obligations. If selected to serve, the candidate's existing and future planned commitments should not materially interfere with board duties. The board may want to know of the candidate's current board memberships. Depending on the company's requirements, a candidate should not be serving on more than four boards (for active CEOs, no more than two). Also, new commitment to serve on the board of another corporation may require board approval.

The motivation to become a director could stem from the potential to network with executives and co-directors, develop or practice leadership skills, improve one's image and gain visibility, and add value to the company. In turn, a directorship could open many other doors.

The director compensation, or fees, could consist of a mix of cash payment and restricted stock units (RSUs), or stock options. Essentially, RSUs are shares of the company that are conditionally restricted for vesting. For example, the director does not earn the RSUs for the fiscal year that he does not serve for the entire period; consequently, the RSUs at year-end do not convert to shares owned by the director at year-end. A stock option is a right in the form of an option given by the company to a director to buy stock in the company (most likely) at a discount. The offering of stock options was a popular means in the past, but has been decreasing in its appeal and usage. Instead, restricted stock units have become more popular.

Besides compensation, one particular benefit a prospective director would look for is insurance coverage for Director and Officer Liability.

With today's proneness of shareholders toward litigation, it is extremely important that board members are protected from risks of litigation where they are not directly liable due to their own action or inaction. Without providing such protection, the company may have difficulty attracting competent director candidates. For this reason, most companies purchase the D&O liability insurance to protect directors from frivolous claims against them. The insurance coverage normally indemnifies the director, officer, or the company for any losses suffered or for defense costs as a result of a legal action, including regulatory investigations or trials, brought for alleged wrongful acts in their capacity as directors or officers. The insurance policy does not cover any penalties agreed upon by the director in lieu of settlement of the charges against the director. The coverage would not apply in cases where the director is at fault and has in fact committed the alleged wrongful acts. While there are companies that would not offer protection through D&O insurance to its directors, it is wise for board candidates to seek such protection. The risk of litigation is high and costs of defending oneself in the event of a legal proceeding could be overwhelming even when you are not at fault.

BIBLIOGRAPHY

Beaudoin, A. M. 2010. The fiduciary duties of directors of for-profit corporations. www.wardandsmith.com/articles/the-fiduciary-duties-of-directors-of-for-profit-corporations, Accessed October 7, 2019.

Block, D. and Gerstner, A. 2016. "One-tier vs. Two-tier board structure: A comparison between the United States and Germany" (2016). Comparative Corporate Governance and Financial Regulation. Paper 1. http://scholarship.law.upenn.edu/fisch_2016/1, Accessed August 30, 2019.

Business Roundtable. 2016. Principles of corporate governance. https://s3.amazonaws.com/brt.org/Principles-of-corporate-governance-2016.pdf, Accessed August 26, 2019.

Deloitte & Touche. 2018. *Audit Committee Resource Guide*. New York: Center for Board Effectiveness.

Larcker, D. F. 2011. *Board of Directors: Duties & Liabilities*. Stanford, CA: Corporate Governance Research Program, Stanford Graduate School of Business.

Murphy, A. 2018. Five essential qualities of a board member. https://greatboards. org/?s=essential+qualities+of+a+director, Accessed October 8, 2019.

Peteghem, M. V., Bruynseels, L. and Gaeremynck, A. 2018. Beyond diversity: A tale of faultlines and frictions in the board of directors. *The Accounting Review* 93(2): 339–367.

Tonello, M. 2019. *The Corporate Board Practices in the Russell 3000 and S&P 500.* Research report R-1687-19-RR. The Conference Board.

CHAPTER **7**

Shareholders

From a corporate governance perspective, a shareholder is an individual or an institution that owns voting shares of the public company. The shareholders take limited risk of ownership while at the same time relegating the duties of management to hired professional hands. They have residual rights to assets of the firm; in case of liquidation of the company, after the creditors are paid the amount owed, the residual amount of resources belongs to the shareholders. From the agency theory perspective, shareholder is the principal and the management, the agent in the principal-agent relationship. Shareholders elect board members to direct and control the management.

SHAREHOLDER DEMOCRACY

Monks and Minow (2011, pp. 140–141) draw an analogy between political democracy and shareholder, or corporate, democracy. While the political democracy guarantees the legitimacy of governmental or public power, corporate democracy harnesses the power of the company management. In the corporate governance arena, shareholders are voters, boards of directors are electoral representatives, proxy solicitation is like an election campaign, and corporate charters, bylaws, and codes operate as constitutions. Like any democracy, the shareholder democracy thrives only if the actors involved are vigilant of their duty and play an active role in the process.

Shareholder democracy is vividly present in how Berkshire Hathaway makes decisions on charitable contributions of the company. Each Berkshire Class A shareholder is able to designate recipients of charitable contributions proportionate to the shareholder's ownership. Shareholder names the charity, Berkshire writes the check, and there are no personal tax consequences on the shareholder. According to Warren Buffett, this is unusual, for the corporation behaves more like a partnership for its philanthropy.

Control through Voting Rights

One share, one vote is generally the norm, giving equal voice to every owner of "a piece of the rock"; the more pieces you own, the greater the number of votes you exercise. In essence, the control is through voting rights. At any given time, the number of shares issued and outstanding determines the aggregate number of votes that could be exercised by the universe of shareholders at that time. Because purchase and sale of shares is ongoing, the number of shareholders changes over time.

Company founders often deliberate over how they would control the company's voting power once it goes public. They would prefer to keep control while going public. For this to happen, they should hold a majority of voting shares; however, this may not be feasible. It may be that the founders don't have the funds to continue to own a majority of voting shares. To get around this challenge, founders may prefer to issue two classes of shares: ordinary shares and super-voting shares. While ordinary shares carry one vote per share, super-voting shares give the investee a multiple number of votes per share, say 30 votes for every share held. As a result, the investors in super-voting shares, typically the founders, executives, and their families, often control the votes and thus ensure that their influence on the company continues to persist while the company enjoys access to public equity market. Fundamentally, the common investor's influence over control and monitoring of the company is marginalized.

There are some benefits of having dual-class equity structure. The founders control the destiny of the company, shielding it from investors who want quick, short-term gains. In this regard, the company enjoys the freedom of a private company. Presumably, the stability of the company and execution of its vision and strategy could remain unperturbed, as in the case of Berkshire, a company with dual-class equity structure. However, there could be disadvantages, too. The company's control could lead management to abuse its power, for example, by making imprudent acquisitions. Shielding itself from any risks of losing control, management may become lax and produce unsatisfactory return on investment, lower sales growth, or higher capital expenditures. In a study of dual- and single-class U.S. corporations, Amoako-Adu and colleagues found that dual-class companies pay out lower cash dividends and repurchase fewer shares. At the heart of the issue lies the motivation and incentives of those with ownership control. However, there is no unequivocal judgment on companies with dual-class shares; some have risen up to the challenge of fiduciary duty to all shareholders, while others have not.

DIVERSITY AMONG SHAREHOLDERS

In the universe of shareholders of a company, there may exist several diverse groups with unique investment objectives of their own. It might be helpful to think of investors as individual investors with limited stakes and institutional investors with potentially significant interests in the ownership of the company. Institutional investors include pension plans, mutual funds, exchange-traded funds, and hedge funds.

Individual Investors

It is conceptually sound and legally proper to describe any investor in a company's shares as a shareholder. Unfortunately, the ownership of a few shares is unlikely to motivate the shareholder to rise up to the spirit of guiding and controlling the management. Even if desired, this may not be possible for a small stock owner, since the number of votes is limited and may not make any difference in the governance decisions. Besides, small holdings may not justify the amount of time or cost involved in exercising vigilance beyond normal reviews of company performance, price fluctuations in the company's share price, and proxy voting. Perhaps because of perceived lack of control over the governance process ("My vote won't count"), most small stock owners may rely on the stock exchange where they would buy and sell shares and determine the timing of such actions. Sometimes labeled as "revolving door" investors, these shareholders may be more market focused; the timing of action (buy, sell, hold) is important to them. This is what they might believe they truly control. In this situation, shareholder rights are not necessarily abrogated, they are merely perceived as ineffective in generating return on their investment, causing inaction on the part of the individual investor.

As such, every investment is truly a risk for the investor, and managing that risk is an important duty of the investor. However, as Monks and Minow explain, in the case of a shareholder, there could be an "ownership failure" due to the difference between the tangible and intangible investments. Take, for example, the owner of a rental property. Wouldn't the owner feel the duty to ensure that rent is collected every month, that the property is not abused by the renter, and that the property does nor remain vacant for a long period of time? Isn't this true regardless of whether the owner hires an agent or does it himself? Because stocks are intangible in some sense, the stockholder could choose to miss the experience of having to actively manage the investment. Not that anyone asks the investor to be passive; if anything, shareholders as investors should be equally vigilant in guarding their investments, exercising the rights assigned to them as owners, and thus controlling risks of the investment.

Institutional Investors

In contrast to individual investors, large stock owners wield proportionately greater influence. These entities in all likelihood have invested in the firm on behalf of other investors, such as employees who subscribe to the pension fund, or the investor who invests in a mutual fund or an exchange-traded fund. For this reason, institutional investors are also called delegated investors who serve as the trustees of the investors. This position of trust puts institutional investors in an additional layer of the principal-agent relationship, representing a large number of investors who contributed to the investment funds. Institutional investors have a duty to vote; they should disclose their voting policy to investors. Their vote probably counts since the institutional investor is often in a relationship with the investee and also has greater voice due to the size of the investment. Their relationship with the investee company is formed by the policies of the institutional investors. For example, they invest for the long haul, exercise due diligence, and support their decisions with considerable analysis of fundamentals of the investee business. Because of the massive number of shares owned, institutional investors wield much greater influence on the board and the company's top executives. It is possible, for example, that an unsatisfied institutional investor may propose their own representatives for election to the board of directors or may push for replacement of the CEO.

Thus, the size of the voting shares held matters. The larger the size, the greater the influence. Because of the size, the returns on their holdings could be better if they make a positive impact on the company's governance actions. Thus, the high stakes of institutional investors in the company invariably tie the future of their financial performance with the company's performance. Therefore, it is likely that institutional investors, individually and collectively, would be more vigilant and active in influencing how well the company is directed and controlled. Perhaps a good barometer of potentially strong governance is the aggregate slice of institutional shareholders in the company's voting shares. The larger the presence of institutional investors, the greater the likelihood that the company is stable and trustworthy.

Even among the institutional investors, the motivations and goals could vary, as could the behavior of the fund manager. While most institutional investors are in it for the long run, there is no assurance that this would happen. A manager of a mutual fund, for example, may lighten up on the fund's investment in a company's shares based on internal evaluation of the company's current condition and future expectations. On the other hand, a manager of an exchange-traded fund (ETF) mimicking an index in her portfolio may not have much flexibility but to remain invested so as to be true to the weights assigned in the index. Hedge funds may be even more volatile as they are focused on targeted returns in the short term and will not remain inactive in the event that things don't go their way!

SHAREHOLDER RETURN ON INVESTMENT

Conceptually, the present value of all anticipated cashflows from an investment in shares is what the shareholder gets in return for the cost of shares. Since cashflows, such as the dividends, occur periodically over time, it is necessary to discount the cashflows using a risk-adjusted rate, called the discount rate. Assume that a shareholder, over the life of his holding, gets four quarterly dividends and obtains cash by selling his shares in the stock market at the year-end. The aggregate present value of all cash inflows (the selling price (net of commissions and charges) at the end of the year and the four dividends at the end of each quarter), compared to the present value of the investment, shows whether the investment yielded the expected return implicit in the discount rate. If the present value of cash inflows is greater (smaller) than the present value of cash outflows, the net present value is positive (negative), suggesting that the return on investment was better (worse) than expected. If the cash-flows are estimates instead of actual amounts, the return calculated is the expected rate of return from the planned investment in shares. Assuming the only goal is the return on investment, the investor would invest in shares only if the risk-adjusted expected rate of return meets the expectations of the investor.

As a practical matter, most individual investors may divide income attributable to shareholders by the amount of stockholder equity to determine their return in a designated time period for which the financial information is compiled. In any case, past performance does not in any way guarantee the future; history may not fully reflect the future potential or upcoming hazards.

Uncertainties Surrounding the Return

Clearly, future cashflows from investment in voting shares are not guaranteed. The board may increase or decrease the dividend distributed, and the share price will most likely vary with the investor expectations of how the company might perform in future. The company may experience a catastrophic cyberattack resulting in data leakage, or some other risks may materialize (e.g., increased cost of foreign sales due to previously unanticipated tariffs, or losses due to currency fluctuations), resulting in losses or reduced profits. During 2017–2019, GE had to cut dividends due to restructuring maneuvers that would shrink the company size and streamline its business segments for future success. The California electric utility PG&E was doing well until the forest fires in some areas caused major problems in 2017 and 2018. State fire investigators concluded that one of the utility's transmission lines sparked the deadliest fire in California. Lawsuits mounted and claims settlements drained resources. According to a Wall Street Journal report, PG&E had recorded by August 2019 wildfire-related charges that in the aggregate exceeded its current market capitalization. As PG&E's experience shows, risks of investing are real and need to be managed all the time.

Company Perspective on Shareholder Returns

A listed public company is going to need new investments from various sources as it grows over time. The company remains an attractive client for financing if its financial health is considered good. A nonperforming company loses the interest of prospective investors and, thus, may sacrifice its market capitalization due to a lower share price. A growing market cap is most likely a healthy sign; the company would be able to borrow funds at attractive rates or issue more shares to generate cash to fund its planned actions. Therefore, satisfied shareholders are important to the company. However, their satisfaction depends on how well the firm is doing financially. This mutuality hinges upon trust in each other. If the shareholders think that the company whose shares they own is going through a tough time but will eventually prevail, chances are, they will not liquidate their investment in the company in the short run.

Institutional investors are often under pressure to generate superior returns on their portfolio of investments. To this end, they want the company to broadcast quarterly earnings guidance and meet or beat the guidance estimates, which may not happen all the time. As Warren Buffett puts it, "earnings simply don't advance smoothly." When the performance falls well below guidance, investors may punish the company by liquidating their investment in it.

Companies attempt to meet investor expectations of return on investment in various ways. For example, the board may declare a stock dividend (dividend in the form of additional shares rather than cash) in times when the company is cash-strapped due to continuing growth. This permits shareholders to sell the extra shares received (or some of the shares they hold) to generate cash, in case they need cash. Companies also declare stock splits, multiplying the number of shares issued and outstanding, thus increasing the number of shares in the hands of a shareholder by a multiple used for the stock split. A stock split potentially increases the mobility of shares in the market, for there are more shares issued and outstanding and each share is more affordable. A stock split would result in at least a temporary reduction in the share price (e.g., a two-for-one split could temporarily result in one-half of the pre-split share price), but if the company is doing well, the share price would likely trend upwards. With more shares on hand, shareholders may sell some and keep the rest, depending on their cash need or alternative investment opportunities.

The board of directors often approves a relatively large budget for the company to purchase its own shares from the open market, especially if the board feels that the shares are undervalued by the market. The share buyback results in fewer shares outstanding, that is, in the hands of shareholders; thus, the participation in the growth of the company belongs to fewer shares, resulting in higher earnings per share and consequently, perhaps higher share price. As a tactic, share buyback is a controversial move, for there are strong pros and cons to the decision to buyback. In the end, however, the goal is to optimize the long-term return to the shareholder. If the company is flooded with cash and has no way to invest the funds profitably, it might as well buy back shares or lighten up on an existing debt.

SHAREHOLDER RIGHTS

As owners, shareholders have specific rights, such as the right to elect board members, to ratify the appointment of independent auditors, approve executive compensation plans, and propose changes to the governance of the company through submission of shareholder proposals. Each is discussed in the following paragraphs.

Election of Board Members

The first and perhaps the most impactful job of investors is to elect their representatives facing the management, the board of directors. This small group of individuals is charged with the accountability to direct and control management's actions with a view to generate long-term shareholder return on their investment in the company. No other duty of a shareholder comes close to this one; if the company is led by weak or submissive directors lacking their own voice, the board could be a totally ineffective agent of the shareholders and management would rule.

The board's governance and nomination committee proposes a slate of board members which is approved by the board. The names of board candidates are included in the proxy ballot for vote by the shareholders. A candidate may be elected by an overwhelming majority, or may struggle to get even a majority of votes cast. The shareholders have the right to vote for a write-in candidate whose name does not appear on the ballot, but for whom the shareholders may vote by writing the person's name. Write-in candidates are uncommon; however, in a proxy fight, a group of investors may suggest the candidacy of someone not on the ballot.

The result of votes cast in the election of directors is only advisory to the board, even where a board candidate does not muster a majority of votes. However, even when these results do not change the board make up, the board should be alert regarding the election outcomes and should consider them in deliberations for preparing a slate of future directors.

Ratification of the Auditor Appointment

The auditor is a coregulator in the company's governance. The assurance of the auditor is the most significant and trusted signal that the financial information shareholders are getting is truthful and fairly presents the financial statements of the company. Therefore, it is essential for the shareholders to ratify the appointment of the external auditors by the audit committee of the board.

The ratification vote is advisory to the board. Even where the ratification fails to muster enough votes, the board may continue to engage the auditor as intended. However, discounting the voice of the shareholders is not in the interest of good governance. The board may have to explain why the auditor appointment is appropriate and how it would take into consideration the shareholders' voice for future auditor appointments.

Approval of Executive Compensation Plan

The agency costs, which include executive compensation, need to be controlled. Hence the shareholders would have a "say on pay" (SOP). The shareholders are asked to approve equity compensation, both short- and long-term, of the senior management, especially the chief executive. Information regarding the executive compensation is usually discussed in the Compensation Discussion & Analysis (CD&A) section of the proxy statement.

Executive compensation has remained a challenge for the board. If the compensation is low relative to management expectations, the executives may leave the company or, if they stay, they may not be motivated to strive for goals that are attainable but challenging. On the other hand, the single most vocal complaint about executive compensation is that the rewards to the management are too high. The board is "giving away the barn."

To determine compensation levels in the best possible manner, the board might retain an outside expert, a compensation consultant who likely has multi-year compensation data for the industry and peer organizations. Besides, the consultant's insights may prove invaluable in doing what is best for the company.

Finally, the approval of compensation by shareholders is required at a frequency determined by the vote of the shareholders. Unless there are any modifications made to the current compensation formula, there may not be any need to discuss compensation every year. The board would desire and anticipate a majority vote in favor of the compensation plan; however, this does not always happen. In the event of a low vote, the board should communicate with the shareholders their position and changes, if any, in their approach going forward.

Shareholder Proposal Submission

Another way that investors may seek to communicate with directors, management, and each other is by submitting shareholder proposals for consideration at the annual meeting. The SEC rules address when a company is required to include a shareholder proposal in its proxy materials. For the shareholder, these rules include both substantive and procedural requirements they must meet:

- The shareholder must own at least one percent of the company's shares, have owned it for a minimum of one year, and will continue to own until the voting date.

- The shareholder is restricted to submit only one proposal.

- The length of the proposal should not exceed 500 words.

- The proposal must not address any prohibited content.

Such proposals cover a spectrum of issues that shareholders are concerned about. They range from ouster of the CEO, executive compensation, board member tenure, environmental concerns, corporate philanthropy, and sustainability, to social issues such as the rights of LGBTQ employees. For example, at its 2019 annual general meeting,

Google's parent company Alphabet faced 13 such proposals, while Amazon had to deal with 12. Here are a few examples:

- Consider separation of the two roles, chairman of the board and the CEO, where the two roles are combined into one position.
- Consider providing a report on sustainability initiatives by the company.
- Realign the chief executive's compensation structure.

Upon receipt of a proposal in proper form and by set due date, the board may place the proposal that meets the requirements in the proxy statement for a nonbinding vote of the shareholder. Normally, the board would append its own understanding of the proposal and what the company is currently working on, or is planning to work on in respect of the issue underlying the proposal. For each proposal under consideration, the board would offer its recommendation regarding whether one should vote for or against the proposal. If a proposal constrains the management's prerogative to run the operations of the company, it would be considered a step toward limiting the management's freedom or micromanaging the company. If such a proposal is included in the proxy, the board recommendation would be to vote against the proposal.

An overwhelming majority of shareholder proposals are rejected. Exceptions are found where a group of shareholders or a hedge fund with an influential amount of voting stock proposes an action. In such cases, however, it may be that the board would work with the proposer in advance of the meeting and arrive at an action plan acceptable to the proposer. For example, in 2019, when Mr. Carl Icahn, who has a 10% stake in the Caesars Entertainment Corp. asked for some changes, the board responded. Caesars replaced three of its board members and gave Mr. Icahn the right to appoint an additional director if a permanent CEO was not named within 45 days of the agreement. Mr. Icahn also asked the company to undertake a thorough strategic review with a view to sell parts of the company or merge businesses to produce greater synergy.

While influential shareholders can express their voice with some degree of ease, other shareholders may be heard as well. Although every shareholder proposal, if voted in, is nonbinding, it does convey to the board and the management what is on the mind of many shareholders. If not directly, the issue underlying the voted and rejected proposal may be addressed by the company in other ways, such as by charting a specific course of action. Over recent years, the shareholder voice via their proposals has become a major force in corporate governance. The issue for the regulators is this: how to empower this force to make it even more effective?

These are routinely acknowledged and honored shareholder rights. But what if shareholders are frustrated about issues that are deemed urgent, need timely response, or just don't neatly fall in any of these rights? They still have various ways in which they could attempt to bring about change. Such actions are discussed in Chapter 12, Shareholder Communication and Engagement.

BIBLIOGRAPHY

Amoako-Adu, B., Baulkaran, V. and Smith, B. F. 2014. Analysis of dividend policy of dual and single class U.S. corporations. *Journal of Economics and Business* 72 (March–April): 1–29.

Blunt, K. and Chin, K. 2019. PG&E losses widen as fire costs rise, Blunt, K. and Chin, K., *The Wall Street Journal*, https://www.wsj.com/articles/pg-e-reports-3-9-billion-in-wildfire-related-charges-11565357268?mod=searchresults&page=1&pos=3, Accessed August 15, 2019.

Buffett, W. 2002. Letter to shareholders. https://www.berkshirehathaway.com/letters/2002.html Accessed October 9, 2019.

Monks, R. A. G. and Minow, N. 2011. *Corporate Governance*. New York: John Wiley & Sons.

CHAPTER 8

Internal Auditing Function

The internal audit function (IAF) is an organizational unit within the company responsible for protecting and enhancing value. It should use a risk-based approach in providing assurance, advice, and insights to the rest of the organization. Broadly, the mission of internal auditing is two-fold: (1) it serves to provide an objective, independent assurance regarding risk management measures, typically recognized as the system of internal controls; and (2) it provides consulting services to the organization in managing risks while adding value.

Often called a watchdog, the IAF in early stages was seen as a cost-center charged with the responsibility of evaluating internal controls in their effectiveness to mitigate risks. The function has progressively gained a higher status. From a focus on internal controls that address risk mitigation, over time, a broader emphasis on risk management became its charge, elevating the function from a cost-center to value-center status. This means that the function is responsible for looking at both the value of a proposed move along with cost-effective management of attendant risks, concurrently addressing opportunity maximization while seeking risk mitigation. In recent times, the function is seen as a governance mechanism, actively engaged in assisting in meeting regulatory compliance requirements.

The current status of the IAF empowers it to engage in Governance, Risk, and Compliance (GRC) in cohort with legal, compliance, risk management, finance, and information technology. The function is poised to fulfill the promise as a guardian of protection from all kinds of risk because of the trust placed in it and the objectivity presumed in its work. GRC, a holistic approach to entity risk management, integrates the internal audit with all related capabilities throughout the organization to manage uncertainty, reduce risk, and leverage opportunities.

PURPOSE

A primary purpose of the IAF is to help the organization manage risk. For this, it should align with the organization's strategy, objectives, and current and evolving risks. Without a clear understanding of the company's business model and how it changes with the execution of its strategy, it would be a challenge for the IAF to achieve effective risk management. This is because a large majority of risks emanate from operations mirrored in the business model. For example, if Walmart adds a self-checkout with the customer's smart phone as a scanner of all products purchased, it would have to identify, evaluate, and address new risks arising from this change in business operations. The potential savings could be significant, but the risks lie in the reliability of the modified system to accurately process the checkout operation.

While core principles of the internal auditing profession remain the same (integrity, competency, objectivity, and confidentiality), types of risks identified and addressed would depend on the nature of the organization, its environment, its business model, and its strategy. An entity that seeks growth through business acquisitions faces quite different risks compared to an entity that seeks organic growth. For example, Facebook's challenges in protecting the privacy of its network users is unique compared to those of IBM, where customers do not pervade in an uncontrolled manner across the business platforms. Where privacy of patron data collides with intelligent online marketing using the same data, anonymity is difficult. And if patrons have considerable influence in protecting their own privacy in such environments, the lack of knowledge or inertia on their part could compromise privacy that Facebook sets out to attain. IBM is not involved in value creation through social marketing. On the other hand, Facebook is deeply engaged in generating revenue through its social network.

Much of the IAF's resources, including time, are devoted daily to controls testing, that is, performing tests of existing controls to assess if they are designed in an effective manner (proper placement, completeness, and reliability of each control, for example) and operate effectively in managing targeted risk(s). If IAF's controls testing work is considered independent, objective, and procedurally sound, the external auditors may also use it as input in their controls testing, a step necessary in their evaluation of effectiveness of the client's internal control system.

Another significant initiative that takes resources of the IAF is the internal consulting of business process owners throughout the organization. Often called Control Self-assessment (CSA), this activity permits the internal auditors to coach, guide, and mentor process owners in the identification of process-based risks and in mitigating them with appropriate controls. The internal consulting activity borders on tasks where the internal auditors could get caught up in their engagement and thus compromise objectivity later when it is time for them to assess independently the controls that process owners use. Ideally, those in the IAF who helped design controls should expect the process owners to implement them and should not subsequently engage themselves in the assessment of effectiveness of these controls. To draw a line between consulting and *independently* testing controls is an important aspect of a successful IAF, for both roles are pivotal. In practice, it seems impossible to permanently designate some auditors as independent and others as non-independent. Consequently, the test of independence is based on the task assigned; the person who provided consultation is considered non-independent for testing the controls that appeared as a result of the consultation.

ORGANIZATION OF THE FUNCTION

The IAF is normally located within the organization at a fairly high level in the hierarchy. Headed by a chief audit executive (CAE), the group collectively would have capabilities necessary to perform its duties well. At the leadership level, staff members may be qualified professionals, such as the CIA, CPA, or CISA. Some may have expertise in forensics, others may be highly technology savvy, still others may be competent in data analytics. The variety of skills needed to perform a specific audit would determine membership of the team that would get the assignment. However, to do this well, it is necessary that the function is adequately staffed with professionals who possess skills likely called upon in an audit.

Since risk management is a high-level responsibility, the leader of the IAF may be a CAE, chief information security officer (CISO), chief risk manager, the CFO, or the CEO. While this accountability structure might be appropriate, it is important to emphasize that for effective governance, management should not be the sole driver of the function. As an agent of the shareholders, the board is responsible to manage risk with a view to protect shareholder interests. In achieving this goal, two main resources available to the board are the IAF and the external auditor. The board and management have more flexibility in shaping what the internal auditors would do, while the external auditor has a well-defined regulatory role as an independent provider of assurance on financial accounting and reporting. To leverage this flexibility with the IAF, the AC of the board must take significant interest in shaping the IAF's agenda and in evaluating the implications of their audit findings. The direct line of accountability to an executive who is part of the management should not inappropriately influence the independence of the internal audit in any form. This can be guarded through active interest of the board, potentially via its AC, in setting the function's agenda and in evaluating from a risk perspective the findings of the IAF.

Outsourcing the IAF

A corporation may outsource the entire function. Due to the critical nature of this decision and its potential impact on governance, the board would be deeply interested in the decision process determining whether to keep inhouse or outsource the IAF. Outsourcing of the IAF may or may not be cost efficient, and not necessarily equally effective. For example, controls testing and risk assessment may be adequately addressed, but the internal consulting and alignment with the company's strategic actions may be minimal due to remoteness of the function. On the other hand, the outsourced function may benefit from the provider's experience with similar organizations, depth in knowledge and expertise, depth and efficiency in controls testing, and insights gained from other clients. If there is management support for outsourcing the function, the AC of the board should take the lead in scope definition, and search, selection, and appointment of the provider organization. The engagement should be reviewed periodically to identify changes to be incorporated in the future as a result of changing structure or objectives of the company. Since this is a non-permissible service for a firm that serves as the company's external auditors, a provider firm must be other than the auditors.

Staffing and Competencies

To do the job well, competent staff should be recruited. Competencies required in the group may change over time as the company goes through transformations via its strategic and tactical moves. Besides, the changing technology and business environment and shifting regulatory requirements warrant that the existing pool of competencies among the staff is evaluated periodically to identify and fill any gaps. For example, intelligent data analytics has surfaced in recent years as an important functional skill for the auditors; this might create the need to recruit new staff, realign the existing staff, or encourage appropriate training among the current group. The staff must be adequate to perform its duties well; shortage could cause trimming of audits that should be done or cutting corners in the audits undertaken. Because the management may consider IAF as simply an overhead depleting the bottom-line, there may be pressure to reduce cost by staffing the function minimally or trimming it to the bone in bad financial times. The board should be cognizant of such tendencies and must voice its opinion when appropriate. The external auditors also have opportunity in their communication with the AC to voice their concern about adequacy, competency, or plans and agenda of the IAF.

There are ways in which the IAF could streamline demands on its resources. For example, many of its routine internal controls testing is on a cycle basis, with high risk cycles being assessed more frequently (e.g., every year) compared to the low risk cycles that are mature, stable, and not subject to material changes that could introduce new risks. Additionally, the auditors use technology (computer aided tools) to reduce time, improve accuracy, and expand the scope (where necessary).

An internal auditor with tenure with the company builds considerable depth in the business processes of the company. As a result, the auditor may recognize a rise in new risks or the sunset of existing risks. An evaluation of such changes could result in adjustments to the current business processes by their owners, thus aligning controls with current risks and perhaps improving business processes as well.

Today's business world is becoming increasingly data-driven. Consequently, auditors will have to continue to hone their skills to conduct business intelligence analytics. The huge amount of qualitative and quantitative data available could be analyzed creatively to produce insights on new risks and how existing risks are mitigated. Additionally, data analytics could help in forensic audits to unearth any compromises or wrongdoings. This is a rather unprecedented development and auditors may have to go through significant continuing education and training to be able to conduct analytics. The challenge is in combining qualitative and quantitative data creatively to produce relevant insights, and this would be possible perhaps by engaging both the right and left brain at the same time!

MANAGING CHANGING RISKS

An effective enterprise risk management must consider change, both internal and external, to the entity. A continual scan of changes will result in significant inputs to the iterative risk evaluation. As a result, controls no longer necessary can be spotted and new controls can be designed and implemented to align with new risks. To illustrate, a corporation that used to offer mailing lists to its customers only by mail launched a new business segment that sold the lists online. Because the business was at the incubation stage, only one person – a young and aspiring woman – was working in this area, defeating the classic mechanism of control through segregation of duties. No new controls were considered for the online sales segment. Under considerable stress to financially help her overspending brother, whom she loved dearly, she started entertaining "sales returns" and granting credit even in cases where there were no real returns; for the fake returns, she used her own credit card to issue refunds, thus pocketing about $220,000 over a period of about 14 months. No one was designated to preapprove granting of such credits and since there was no inventory coming back to the company (what was sold was a digital list), additional possible controls to verify sales returns were also missing. Had the internal audit function noticed the launch of a new segment and evaluated new risks in it, they could have easily suggested that the only credit card acceptable for refund is the card used to pay for the order! An Oracle programmer detected the compromise when he noticed frequent refunds issued on the same credit card. The lesson is simple: if a business segment is new and growing, its evaluation by the board, the CFO, the internal auditors, and the external auditors should not only be in terms of profitability and growth, but also the attendant risks and how they are currently mitigated.

It is important to recognize that the organization and its environment is subject to constant change. For example, the "Uberization" of the hospitality industry has caused considerable shifts in how the traditional hotel-motel companies, such as the Hilton, would respond, and the fintech revolution has caused the financial services industry (and specifically, credit card companies) to address how they would participate in the new shape of payment processing online. The bitcoin revolution, although going through some rough spots, could stabilize over time and create even more shifts in the way banks manage currency and process payments. It appears applications of the blockchain technology, driverless cars, and drone deliveries are just around the corner! Such changes could bring about changes in the business model and business processes affecting the risk scenarios and risk mitigation measures. To survive, the businesses of yesterday may adopt innovations in their industry or risk losing their competitive strength.

In addition to the challenges of survival, businesses are constantly facing cybersecurity threats. The SEC has mandated that public companies should discuss in their annual report (10K) the risks of cybersecurity, actual incidences of such attacks, and how well the company is prepared to protect itself from such attacks. The evidence shows that companies either do not discuss the matter or minimally address it in their annual report, often using a boilerplate description. From a governance viewpoint, this is a significant event in the life of a company, for any disclosure of such disruption potentially has a market price effect on the shares of the company. It is incumbent upon the board to determine if its 10K filing includes the discussion of cyberattacks experienced by the company and how the company manages to protect itself from such attacks.

Setting Priorities

Depending on the company size, the internal audit resources may or may not be able to afford all of the competencies essential for the entity's risk management. For example, it may not be possible for even a large company to have on board a staff capable of performing an operating systems audit. In such cases, the management may retain a consultant to do the job. Moreover, there are situations where the board may prefer to seek help from an outside expert who (1) is independent, (2) can be objective on critical issues facing the company, and (3) will not cause disruption in the internal auditing plans. To illustrate, if a company is wrapped up in significant related-party transactions, an opinion of a professional otherwise not connected with the company should help understand and address the impending dilemma. Another situation where an outside expert could provide insights is where the company CEO is using chartered flights, where some personal use might be involved. Accounting for and reporting of benefits related to the personal use of company aircraft is an issue on which internal staff may have limited knowledge, experience, or insights. Shopping for an assurance on such issues requires the provider to have near-total independence and depth in competencies called for in the assignment. In sum, the board has considerable powers to call for resources it deems essential in performing its duties.

COSO CONTROL FRAMEWORK

The Committee of Sponsoring Organizations (COSO), following a recommendation of the Treadway Commission, studied the domain of internal controls in a comprehensive manner. The COSO study resulted in an integrated framework of internal controls, called the COSO framework. Discussed briefly in Chapter 3, this framework proposes five components of internal controls: risk assessment, control environment, control activities, information and communication, and monitoring. Each component is articulated below.

Risk Assessment

An entity exists to achieve its objectives. It may not achieve these objectives because there are risks involved along the path to its success. For each risk identified at all levels within an organization, several questions should be asked: what is the nature of the risk? What is the likelihood that it will actually materialize? What is the benefit of managing the risk? What are the alternative ways in which the risk can be managed and what is the expected cost of each? This process of identification and evaluation of risk and determination of appropriate processes to control it is called risk assessment.

Control Environment

If the leadership of an entity does not have an appropriate control mindset, often called "tone at the top," any control processes set up within the organization will become more like rituals, leading to less than effective control. The board of directors, management's philosophy and operating style, organizational structure, assignment of authority and responsibility, and human resources policies and procedures are key factors in assessing the control environment of an entity. The control environment provides organization-wide discipline and structure and influences and permeates the other components of the internal control system.

An elaborate risk assessment process still will be ineffective if the mindset of the leadership does not support and promote it. Therefore, risk assessment begins with an assessment of the control environment. Where the control environment is unfit to support a system of internal controls, risk assessment and the components that follow it will have little influence.

Control Activities

Having identified risks in achieving objectives, the next question is: how are these risks going to be managed? Necessary actions to manage the identified risks should be determined. These actions are then "embedded" into policies and procedures of the organization to help ensure these actions will take place as part of the processes of the entity.

An internal control is essentially a representation of control activity. At the operational level, internal controls are an integral part in the transactions of an organization. Since the nature and classes of transactions vary across organizations, internal controls are unique to the transaction stream. For example, returns of merchandise by customers need careful inspection prior to accepting the return in accordance with the store policy. Depending on the store policy, affiliates who sell merchandise may not be involved in accepting returns from customers. The segregation of

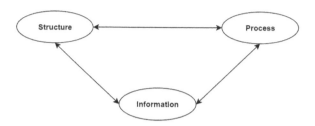

FIGURE 8.2 Relationship between process, structure, and information in a control activity.

AUDIT PLANNING

Simply, an audit plan is a collection of all planned internal audit engagements for a period of time. This collection of audit engagements is carefully derived following a review of recent changes in the organization, major transactions (such as business acquisitions), industry-specific changes, and changes in regulatory requirements. Business processes are evaluated in terms of risk levels and new risks in order to determine which audits rise up to the level of "important" or "important and urgent." Besides, there usually are audits that are scheduled on a cyclical basis so as to cover the universe of all critical business processes over a period of years. In addition to existing business processes, the information technology initiatives of the entity may result in new or improved processes and these need to be evaluated within a short time frame to assure reliable and relatively risk-free operations.

The IAF serves two purposes: as an internal consultant to process owners and as an auditor of internal controls. The latter focuses on regulatory compliance, although its major contribution is toward risk management for the company. The board is certainly interested in both purposes and exerts forceful oversight on both, especially the latter. Management has certainly equal if not more interest in process improvements while mitigating risks; this will help lower the cost of doing business while at the same time improving the overall experience of the stakeholders (customers, suppliers, employees, etc.) of the process. Whereas the board is not against improvements, it would not want to over-allocate resources of the internal audit toward this purpose at the cost of marginalizing the compliance efforts. A delicate balance in the allocation of the IAF resources between the two broad objectives of the IAF should be maintained to gain the most out of limited resources.

It is important for the board and its AC to see that the IAF provides room for ongoing projects that involve new risks to the company and that management takes advantage of such opportunity to seeking help in the assessment of emerging risk. To illustrate, Hewlett-Packard acquired a British company for several billion dollars only to find out in about a year's time that much of the value of the acquisition did not materialize. This resulted in a write down of the assets acquired. A primary cause of the shocking revelation was that the acquired company's executive presented falsified information to Hewlett-Packard. This could have been averted if in its due diligence process, the company had involved the IAF to investigate the veracity of data presented by the acquired company. Such forensic investigation could help avoid all the energies spent on a fruitless M&A effort. And even assuming that the IAF, upon its investigation, gave a "clean bill of health" to the business being acquired, the learning on the part of the internal audit would help greatly in managing the risks of integrating the acquired company into the acquiring entity. The CFO, CISO, and the board should insist on due diligence of all new and material risks arising from the management's strategic, tactical, and operational decisions.

Returning to the audit engagements, the internal audit function would typically evaluate controls in business processes relevant to the organizational function, such as procurement or payroll. Figure 8.3 presents the steps to determine if controls are working. Tests of controls, also called compliance tests, result in one of three outcomes:

- There may be minor internal control irregularities, with a near-normal state of risk management.

- A deficiency, or a combination of deficiencies, in an internal control may be less severe than a material weakness (see below), yet important enough to address by the process owner.

- A deficiency, or a combination of deficiencies, that increase the probability of a potential misstatement of financial statements is called material weakness. This means that the controls in place are ineffective and must be corrected in the near term.

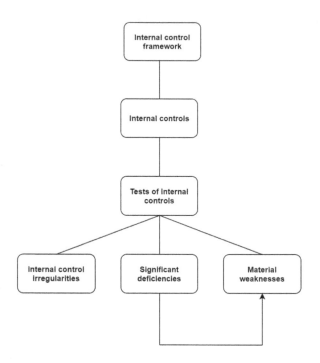

FIGURE 8.3   Tests of internal controls.

Furthermore, a collection of significant deficiencies could result in a material weakness. All irregularities must be shared as feedback to the process owners, with priority set for correction of material weaknesses. A follow up by the IAF and perhaps controls re-testing is essential to get the assurance that the identified weaknesses are corrected and the process is under control.

Relationship with External Auditor

In addition to those in charge of governance, a major beneficiary of the internal audit's work is the external auditor. In the process of evaluating the internal control system, the external auditor may rely on the controls testing work of the internal auditor, provided that such work is properly planned, executed, and well-documented. In controls testing, the internal auditor should mirror independence from the management; absence of independence may make the work unusable by the external auditors.

The use of internal auditors' work by independent auditors also is a benefit to the company. A greater reliance on the IAF's work would mean less effort for the external auditors and thus, lower audit fees for the company. For this to occur, the IAF must share its audit plan and regularly communicate with the external auditor to develop mutual trust and work collaboratively where the needs of the two auditors overlap. Finally, it would be beneficial for the company to share with auditors the findings of outside consultants retained to investigate special issues, such as related-party transactions or cybersecurity threat assessment.

GOVERNANCE AND THE INTERNAL AUDIT FUNCTION

For the board, especially its audit committee, the reliance on the IAF is crucial. Without the IAF's work, it would not be possible to ascertain if the controls are working and whether regulatory requirements are met. The reports of the IAF should be timely, organizationally focused, and actionable. While independent auditors' opinions matter, it is the internal audit that could greatly help them reach an opinion that represents high quality and low costs. Without a strong presence of the IAF, an independent auditor may be hard to recruit, and even if a public accountant agrees to fill the role, it would be an expensive experience for the board.

BIBLIOGRAPHY

Brender, N. and Gauthier, M. 2018. Impacts of blockchain on the auditing profession. *ISACA Journal* 5: 27–32.

Morse, E. A., Raval, V. and Wingender, J. R., Jr. 2017. SEC cybersecurity guidelines: Insights into the utility of risk factor disclosures for investors. *The Business Lawyer*, Winter 2017–18.

Raval, V. and Acharya, P. 2019. Today's interdisciplinary auditors. *The ISACA Journal* 5: 14–18.

Raval, V. and Dentlinger, M. J. 2017. Risk landscape of driverless cars. *EDPACS* 56(3): 1–18.

Raval, V. and Fichadia, A. 2007. *Risks, Controls, and Security*. New York: John Wiley & Sons.

Raval, V. and Jalan, C. 2018. Mergers and acquisitions, should internal audit be involved in due diligence? *ISACA Journal* 5: 13–16.

Raval, V., Morse, E. A. and Wingender, J. R., Jr. 2011. Market price effects of data security breaches. *Information Security Journal: A Global Perspective* 20: 263–273.

CHAPTER 9

Financial Reporting and External Auditing

The external auditor is an outside, independent provider of assurance about fairness of financial results. Independent of management and outside of its control, the external auditors can exert significant influence in their assessment of the quality of financial information produced and disseminated to interested parties, including the shareholders. As a result of the audit, they express an opinion on the fairness of management's process of generating financial information and would thus communicate if the results of the financial accounting and reporting system of the company are fairly presented.

For the board and all parties interested in corporate governance, independent auditors are practically the coregulators. As coregulators, they fill a crucial role that no one else is charged with. Trust in independent auditors is what makes them not just another service provider, but rather a partner in the process of governing the company. Stemming from independence, competencies and skills, and professionalism and ethics, their view of the company's financial accounting and reporting system is invaluable in company governance.

FINANCIAL ACCOUNTING

In order to understand what the auditors do, it is first necessary to have a broad understanding of what a financial accounting system is and what financial statements are prepared using this system. Financial accounting systems process economic transactions of the company, using generally accepted accounting principles (GAAP) usually set by an independent standard-setting body, such as the Financial Accounting Standards Board (FASB) in the U.S.A. Transactions are typically classified using activities, such as those relating to operations, investment, and financing. Logically, transactions mirror activities that trigger the economic impact on the firm.

When the company's transactions for a period of time are processed, the aggregate economic impact of such transactions is distilled in several different financial statements, such as the income statement, the balance sheet, and the statement of cash flows. The income statement summarizes the flow of income over a period of time. The balance sheet reports the state of assets, liabilities and stockholders' equity as of a specific date, and the statement of cash flows summarizes the flow of cash over a period of time, classified into one of three categories: cash flow from operations, cash flow from investing activities, and cash flow from financing activity. Because financial statements condense diverse, complex activities using a double-entry financial accounting model, much of the qualitative information, such as accounting policies of the company, is shared in the footnotes to the financial statements.

Selected accounting principles and statements are discussed in Table 9.1 and a high-level concept map of the accounting process is shown in Figure 9.1. Any entity's assets, or resources, equal claims against these assets. The claims, also called equities, are of two types, debt (borrowed money) and stockholders' equity (invested money). The stockholders' equity consists of capital contributions by the shareholders and retained earnings. The retained earnings equal accumulated income (revenues minus expenses) over the life of the entity, less dividends declared by the board. This is accumulated income, net of dividends declared, retained by the entity.

Accounting for complex transactions in a large public company would involve considerable judgments by management, including in the use of estimates. Thus, the accounting system that generates financial numbers is complex and requires the auditors to have significant depth in the audit client's industry and business model as well as preferences of management where the accounting standards provide alternative ways of treating financial transactions. The auditors' brief

TABLE 9.1 Selected accounting principles and statements
___

Income, also referred to as earnings, equals revenue minus expenses. Revenues are increases in resources that arise from the products or services provided by the firm. Revenues must be recognized in the period in which they are earned, no matter when they are received. Expenses are decreases in resources of a firm in the process of earning revenues. Expenses should be recognized when incurred, not when paid. Expenses should be matched against the revenues such expenses generated in the period. Thus, a period of time for which revenues and expenses are measured is an important consideration, because expenses, even if not paid in the period, should be recorded in the period where they belong, that is, the period in which such expenses directly or indirectly helped generate the revenues earned. The violation of matching of expenses against revenues would result in an inconsistent measurement of income.

Because shareholders bear the risk of owning the firm, any income earned increases the stockholders' claim against the resources of the firm, called stockholders' equity. Income earned and accumulated (that is, not distributed to the shareholders as dividends, for example) is called the retained earnings. The stockholders' equity is reported in two major categories: retained earnings and contributed capital (e.g., money received from shareholders at the time of issue of shares). Changes in stockholders' equity are reported in the statement of changes in stockholders' equity.

The accounting model is simple: Assets = Liabilities + Stockholders' Equity. Assets are economic resources, owned or controlled by the firm, that will provide future benefits and can be reliably measured. Example of assets include cash, equipment, cars, and land. Liabilities are obligations (or debts) arising from past transactions that the firm must pay, in money or services, sometime in the future. When assets, liabilities and stockholders' equity balances are presented at a point in time, say, December 31, the statement thus prepared is called the balance sheet. By design, the balance sheet must always "balance," that is, total assets must equal the sum of liabilities and stockholders' equity.

In preparing the income statement, revenues must be reported when earned and expenses should be matched against revenues. Expenses are thus reported in the period in which they are incurred in generating revenues of the period. As a result, cash inflows (e.g., revenues received) and outflows (e.g., expenses paid) are most likely different than revenues earned, whether received or not, and expenses incurred, whether paid on not, for the same period. After all, changes in cash are concrete – objective, verifiable, and beyond any assumptions or estimates – and therefore, investors would prefer to learn about the changes in cash over a fiscal year (a 12-month period the firm chooses to report its financial performance). The statement that reports the changes in cash and cash equivalent from the beginning to the end of the period is called the statement of changes

(Continued)

TABLE 9.1 (Cont.)

in cash, or the cash flow statement. The changes reported are categorized as operating, investing, and financing cash flows.

To summarize, the revenue recognition principle requires that revenues should be recognized in the period in which they are earned, regardless of when they are received. The matching principle warrants the all expenses incurred, no matter when paid, should be reported in the period incurred, thus matching expenses against revenues for the period. The periodicity principle requires that the firm's lifespan should be divided into 12-month periods, called fiscal years. The income statement, the statement of changes in stockholders' equity, and the statement of cash flow should be prepared for each fiscal year and the balance sheet should be prepared at the end of each fiscal period.

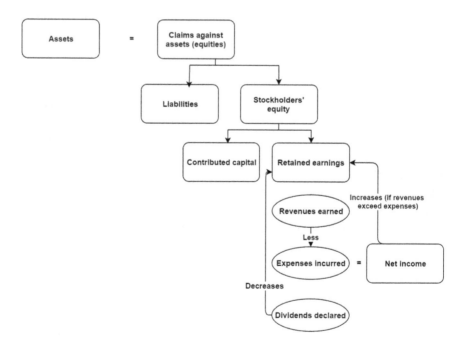

FIGURE 9.1   The financial accounting process.

letter expressing their opinion does not fully reflect how elaborate and complex the audit process is for most public companies. We examine in the following paragraphs how the auditor facilitates the governance process.

EXTERNAL AUDITORS AND THE GOVERNANCE PROCESS

A primary goal of the external audit is to seek assurance that the financial statements prepared by management are truthful. For this assurance, the board and the shareholders engage a public accountant or a public accounting firm. To ensure that the audit was done without any intervention by management, the external auditor reports to the board of directors, the body that represents shareholders of the company. As a result, all matters related to the external auditors – appointment, determination of audit fees, communication of results of the audit, etc. – are the responsibility of the audit committee of the board. As such, the core purpose of having an audit committee is to provide an oversight on the accounting and financial reporting system of the company and on the audits of the system and its outputs. In the unlikely event that such a committee does not exist, the entire board is the primary group managing the relationship with the company's auditors.

What do the external auditors do? To understand their role as coregulators in the governance process, it is important to discuss the nature of external audit.

EXTERNAL AUDIT

Shareholders have no direct access to financial information. Such information is disseminated to them in presentations of the board and management of the company, via conference calls, for example. Financial statements at the end of each quarter (10Qs) and at the end of the company's fiscal year (10K) are filed with an appropriate regulatory agency, such as the SEC in the USA. The auditors review quarterly statements and audit the annual statements with a view to provide an audit opinion. There are three specific threads to the auditors' opinion:

1. An opinion regarding whether the financial information is presented fairly in conformity with the GAAP.

2. An opinion on management's assessment of the effectiveness of the design and operation of internal control over financial reporting.

3. For large public companies, an opinion on the effectiveness of internal control.

If the internal controls involved in the systems that generate financial information are absent or weak, the system is vulnerable to risks such as the risk of inaccurate input or incomplete transaction processing. Therefore, management is required to monitor the internal controls related to the financial accounting and reporting system and to express an opinion on how well these controls are designed and if they operate effectively. In turn, the auditors are required to express an opinion on management's assertion about the quality of internal controls.

Compliance and Substantive Testing

Financial audits require nearly year-round activities. Some audit activities, called compliance testing, have to do with (1) testing controls surrounding the *process* which generates financial information, while (2) other audit activities, called substantive testing, focus on the financial information as such, for example, transaction testing and the verification of account balances (e.g. cash balance at year-end). Controls surrounding the process are crucial to ensure that the process works reliably. Compliance testing of these controls can occur on a year-round cycle rather than as an end-of-year exercise. If controls cannot be trusted, then the content that the system processes to produce financial information may not be trustworthy. To express an opinion on the content under such condition, considerably more testing of transactions and account balances should be undertaken.

Substantive testing has to do with substance or result of financial transactions. Much of the verification of results of financial transactions can be done only after the fiscal year-end. Therefore, activities related to the actual content of the financial statements, such as verification of cash balance at year-end, is undertaken as part of substantive testing of transactions and account balances.

Finally, the internal audit as a risk management function is much more involved in compliance testing and may only incidentally engage in tests of transactions and account balances. Because the external auditors have to do controls testing independently, they do benefit from the findings of the internal auditors regarding the effectiveness of financial accounting and reporting controls. This is where most overlap between the internal and external auditing would likely occur.

Audit Scope

At a minimum, the scope of the audit is guided by what is required and must be complied with under the current regulations. Three quarterly reviews and the annual audit are central in the scope of the audit. The objectives of the audit, responsibility of the external auditor, responsibility of management, and the extent and type of reliance on the work of IAF are distinctly articulated in the engagement letter. Clearly, the scope determines the overall boundaries of audit engagement and must be carefully evaluated by the AC and, as well, discussed with the prospective external auditors at the time of recruiting the auditor.

Subject to approval by the AC (usually the chair of the committee), certain permissible non-audit services can be procured by the client company from the external auditors. Practically, it makes sense to engage the auditors to help the company where, because of their audit work and professional background and experience, they are poised to contribute effectively. For example, the auditors may be retained for tax services or for helping with the due diligence of an acquisition under consideration by the audit client. Caution must be exercised by the AC in approving such additional services. For example, a careful evaluation of the effect of the services being approved on the independence of the auditors should be undertaken prior to approval of services.

Recognizing that small companies will find these requirements rather an expensive burden on their profitability, the SEC has recommended that companies with an annual revenue of $100 million or less will not have to have an external auditor to provide assurance on the financial statements. While this may be a relief to small businesses, the downside is that it is usually the small companies where it is likely that controls are ineffective or absent and financial frauds could occur.

Distinction Between Review and Audit

As to the output of financial systems, the auditors typically "review" the financial statements quarterly and "audit" the statements prepared for the fiscal year. In a review, the auditors aim to provide a limited level of assurance that the financial statements presented by the management do not require material modifications. Using analytical procedures, auditors seek comfort that relationships among the financial data of the period under review are consistent with the history of the company. Audit procedures used in a review are "light," and the auditors' reliance on the management representations is high.

In an audit, the audit procedures are significant and comprehensive. The auditors use several additional procedures, such as the examination of source documents, third-party verification of account balances, physical inspection of assets, and tests of internal controls. The level of assurance provided is low in a review, high in an audit; and the type of assurance provided is negative (not aware of any material problems or issues) in a review, positive (statements are a fair presentation) in an audit. Consequently, the audit is a much more rigorous exercise, heavy in time and resource consumption, compared to the review. If the same audit firm repeats the review and audit process year-after-year, their understanding of and experience with the client's risks and systems would generate efficiencies, and therefore lower costs, over time. However, one concern is that a longer auditor tenure could blunt auditor independence.

THE AUDITING PROFESSION

Prior to the enactment of the SOX, the profession of auditing was self-regulated. The AICPA guided the development and use of auditing standards to its membership. Even today, the AICPA is responsible for auditing standards that apply to non-public companies, such as the private companies. However, with the arrival of SOX, a non-profit entity under the oversight of the SEC was formed. The overriding purpose of this entity, called the Public Company Accounting Oversight Board (PCAOB), was to stem the erosion of public trust and investor confidence in audit quality and generally, the audit profession. The PCAOB oversees the audits of public companies (including the SEC-registered brokers and dealers) with the aim to protect investors and further the public interest enhanced by the preparation of informative, accurate, and independent audit reports. The PCAOB (1) exercises due diligence to register external auditors serving, or planning to serve, public companies; (2) conducts inspections of public company audits; (3) establishes standards related to auditing; and (4) investigates compromises or impropriety where it deems warranted.

The loss of power to set their own auditing standards has been considered a setback for the accounting profession. While the profession, through its main bodies, has potential to provide input and share insights, the final decision on audit standards rests with the PCAOB. Lawmakers have voted on an independent standard-setting body presumably to reestablish trust in the audit process and its results. It may have little to do with possible conflict of interest as a self-regulator.

Two relevant sets of standards have to do with financial accounting and auditing. Consider first the accounting standards, also called U.S. GAAP, or generally accepted accounting principles. Under the umbrella of the AICPA since 1959, the accounting principles board promulgated accounting standards. An independent body, the FASB was created under the umbrella of the Financial Accounting Foundation in 1973. Since then, the FASB has been accountable for developing financial accounting and reporting standards. The SEC endorses the FASB standards; however, occasionally, if an interested party (e.g., preparers of financial statements) has concerns about a new standard, the SEC would make the final call. The AICPA has been an influential body in the standard-setting process followed by the FASB.

As discussed earlier, the auditing standards were previously promulgated by the AICPA; the PCAOB took over the responsibility for setting public company auditing standards since its formation in 2002. A schematic view of the auditing profession is provided in Figure 9.2.

QUALIFICATIONS OF EXTERNAL AUDITORS

Qualified auditors have earned a professional certification, Certified Public Accountant (CPA) in the USA, have an active license to practice as an auditor, and are registered with the PCAOB as an individual or as a member of a public accounting firm. In essence, the auditors should meet the requirements of competency and independence. Unless the

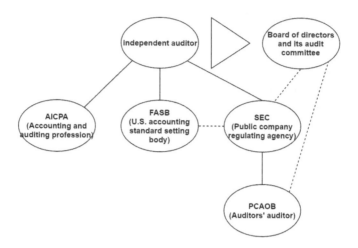

FIGURE 9.2   The auditing profession.

auditor has an adequate comprehension of the accounting standards and how to apply them, it would be a challenge to provide the required opinion. The auditor should also be quite conversant with the risks involved in the audit engagement and how these risks can be and are addressed. These risks include not just the risk inherent in the audit process, but also the risks in the client systems, operations, and external environment. The auditor should also be an effective communicator, project manager, and above all, a person with a high level of integrity.

External auditors must also be independent. Independence of mind is important; it is operationally supported by measures such as leaving no conflicts of interest, direct or remote, with the audit client. The greater the conflict of interest, the lower the perceived degree of auditor independence. For example, the auditor should have no direct invest-ment in the client company, nor should any person related to the auditor have any interest in the company, as a key employee or a supplier, for example. Independence is presumably compromised if the auditor stays in this role for a period of time or negotiates a contingent fee for the audit; it also is presumably compromised if past due fees for audit services exist. While each of these measures help to contribute toward maintaining independence, ultimately, the person's integrity drives effective exercise of independence.

Under PCAOB Rule 3526(b), auditors must at least annually provide audit committee members with sufficient information to understand how a relationship between the auditor and the audit client might affect the auditor's independence. Specifically, the audit firms must:

- Provide a written description of all relationships that may reasonably be thought to bear on independence, between the firm, including its affiliates, and the audit client, together with persons in financial reporting oversight roles at the audit client;

- Discuss with the audit committee of the audit client the potential effects of the relationships;

- Affirm to the audit committee the firm's compliance with PCAOB Rule 3520, *Auditor Independence* (Rule 3520); and

- Document the substance of its discussion with the audit committee of the audit client.

AUDITOR SELECTION, APPOINTMENT, AND COMPENSATION

An audit engagement is a two-way process: the public accountant should be willing to take the engagement, and the company should be willing to appoint the public accountant in the auditor role. The thought that a public accounting firm would accept any company as its clients is impractical. There may be a variety of reasons not to sign an engagement letter with certain companies. For example, if the firm has a large client (e.g., Coca Cola Company) in the same industry space, it may have to resist accepting another large client (e.g., Pepsi) in the same space, for fear of loss of confidentiality. If the firm is providing significant non-audit services to the company that could no longer be offered upon taking the audit engagement, there might be a net revenue foregone in accepting the audit. The audit risk that the prospective client renders is a factor as well; high risk companies may be avoided by firms that already have significant clientele with manageable risk levels. Upon the enactment of SOX, the Big Four dropped from their audit engagements many client companies deliberately, for their work on the

The Role of Management in the Audit Process

Whereas the AC is in direct communication with the auditors, it is important to recognize that the bulk of the audit work happens with significant interaction between management and the auditors. It is often clarified that the financial information is that of management, not of auditors. Management is responsible for the financial statements and should fully engage with the auditors. Management should ensure that there is no obstruction in the audit and that the auditors are provided with information that management generated. The auditors, for example, would need access to data and information systems, systems documentation, accountants and other employees of the company, legal counsel, and the treasurer. Management has to coordinate such requests from the auditors, answer questions that arise during the audit, and furnish additional information that auditors ask for.

During the audit, differences may surface between how management has accounted for certain transactions and how the auditors believe such transactions should be accounted for according to the GAAP. Such differences, normally called audit differences, should be discussed and resolved between the auditor and management; any remaining material differences (along with the differences resolved with management) are presented by the auditors to the AC, with a clear communication regarding the impact of unresolved differences, if any, on the audit opinion.

Any disagreements with management about matters, whether or not satisfactorily resolved, could be individually or in the aggregate, significant to the company's financial statements and perhaps may have an impact on the content of the auditor's report. Aside from the content, any difficulties encountered during the audit (e.g., significant delays by management to provide information needed for the auditor to perform his or her audit procedures) may result in scope limitation, modified opinion, or withdrawal from the engagement.

Communication with the Audit Committee

AS 1301 specifies the requirements regarding auditor communication with the AC. These include, but are not limited to:

- matters related to the conduct of an audit (the responsibilities of the auditor in relation to the audit);

- overall strategy and timing of the audit;

- timely communication of observations arising from the audit;

- significant issues that the auditor discussed with management, including the application of accounting principles and auditing standards, critical accounting policies and practices that are both (1) most important to the portrayal of the company's financial condition and results and (2) require management's most difficult, subjective, or complex judgments, and;

- critical accounting estimates made in accounting and financial reporting.

The auditor must obtain certain information from the audit committee relevant to the audit, for example, any knowledge on the part of the AC regarding violations or possible violations of laws or regulations, or any occurrence of financial fraud.

AUDIT REPORT

An overwhelming majority of audit opinions issued by public accountants are what are called unqualified opinion. Key contents of such an opinion are discussed in Table 9.2. In essence, "present fairly" signifies the use of financial accounting standards. Additionally, management as the preparer of financial statements is distinguished from the auditor who expresses an opinion on these statements. Other types of opinion are:

- Qualified opinion: when the financial statements reflect departure from the GAAP, or there is a lack of evidence or the scope of the audit is restricted, the auditor would cite these exceptions to an otherwise "clean" opinion.

- Adverse opinion: where the statements taken as a whole are not presented fairly in accordance with the GAAP.

- Disclaimer of opinion: where an accurate opinion couldn't be formed for a variety of reasons (e.g., missing financial records), the auditor chooses to disclaim an opinion.

are appointed to offer an opinion on the company's financial statements. This is why they are called coregulators; no one can fill their role in the governance process.

The acknowledgment of the indispensable role of the auditor does not imply the absence of hurdles. Auditors sometimes fail in their oversight and due diligence. For example, in the audit of global corporations, the auditor may rely on local affiliates whose work may not be at par with the expectations. Also, in the vast amount of financial records, the auditors can examine only a limited amount of evidence with the possibility that unidentified problem areas are not adequately examined.

Fiscal compromises present in the conduct of a company, if not noticed by the auditors, could do considerable damage over a long period of time. Others might detect such compromises in the line of duty, but may not report them for fear of backlash. In the case of Satyam Computers, for example, the multi-year manipulation of financial information was not revealed until the fraudster himself, the chairman of the board and co-founder of the company, admitted to the wrongdoing. Misrepresentation and financial fraud are here to stay. The number of restatements of financial statements is astounding and continues to plague the financial world. The auditors are the best source of protection for the shareholders; ongoing efforts to improve the audit quality can only help to enhance the profession's invaluable work.

BIBLIOGRAPHY

Deloitte & Touché. 2018. *Audit Committee Resource Guide.* New York: Center for Board Effectiveness.

PCAOB. 2017. The auditor's report on an audit of financial statements when the auditor expresses an unqualified opinion. June 1, 2017. https://pcaobus.org/Standards/Auditing/Pages/AS3101.aspx, Accessed October 17, 2019.

PCAOB. 2019. Implementation of critical audit matters: The basics, staff guidance. March 18. https://pcaobus.org/Standards/Documents/Implementation-of-Critical-Audit-Matters-The-Basics.pdf, Accessed October 17, 2019.

III

Governance in Action

CHAPTER 10

The Board in Action

The board has to balance its oversight efforts between two areas: compliance and performance. It is management that bears the charge of being compliant and delivering performance; the board is supposed to monitor management. However, such clear lines are difficult to draw in practice. How do you know if you, as a director, are overstepping into management's territory?

Since management is accountable for the company's performance, there is a fine line drawn between oversight and actual management of the company. There is some degree of discretion here as to the extent to which the board would step on management's turf; it seems likely that the more management fails to perform well, the more likely it is that the board would reinforce its oversight function. This could go in the other direction as well: the more effective management in delivering results, the greater the risk that the board would fall asleep in its vigilance over management. In such cases, powerful chief executives could amass unchallenged influence in what they want to do, sometimes at the risk of organizational wrongdoing. The Wells Fargo Corporation, once a hallmark of excellence, is still suffering from its woes of irregularities and unethical conduct in aggressive pursuit of business growth.

The other area is compliance. In this regard, the board generally draws a hard line. It is unlikely to accept any misses on the part of management with respect to compliance with regulatory requirements. Respect for laws and regulations in all aspects of the company's dealings is a threshold that should be met, no exceptions. However, even here, management's errors and omission can surface, especially if senior management garners unquestionable dominance. Volkswagen's emission control workarounds have caused serious damage to a once invincible motor company with high integrity.

COMPLIANCE

Much of what is disclosed to the shareholders and media generally has to do with compliance – compliance with numerous regulations. For example, if the company is providing information technology outsourcing services, it is likely that the data centers and technologists are located in various parts of the world. Depending on projects and clients in the United States, for example, the company would send to the USA personnel needed to cater to client projects. For entry in the USA for business, a special kind of visa is necessary. Procurement of such visas and compliance with related regulatory requirements is essential for the company; without it, interruptions in service to the client may occur, the business reputation could be damaged, and client interest in the company would dissipate. The company's board should carefully review how well management is complying with immigration requirements. Similarly, mobile phone companies are responsible for meeting the requirements of the Federal Communications Commission (FCC) and a retail grocery chain would have the Food and Drug Administration's (FDA) requirements to meet. The load of compliance comes from different regulators depending on the nature of business and types of risks involved.

An important source of regulatory requirements for public companies originates from the Securities & Exchange Commission (SEC) in the USA. The company needs to file with the SEC many different forms to communicate through the SEC's website various information to investors. For example, Form 10Q is used to file quarterly financial statements, and 10K for annual reports. Form 8K is used to convey various changes, for example, director resignation. Proper and timely filing of these forms is important for the survival of the company. Without meeting such baseline requirements, the company may run into significant distractions from its operating goals and perhaps legal trouble, and could even face bankruptcy in severe situations.

Following the tech-bubble bust in 2001, the U.S. lawmakers enacted the Sarbanes-Oxley Act (SOX), the law named after its two sponsors.

Crisis in the financial markets in 2007–2008 brought an additional deluge of requirements through the passage of the Dodd-Frank Act (The Wall Street Transparency and Accountability Act of 2010). With these two laws and related regulatory requirements, the pendulum swung toward a degree of over regulation. The Trump Administration recognized that a heavy dose of regulation may have caused companies to be bogged down with compliance requirements, spending more time and money, and perhaps even getting distracted from the strategic, tactical, and operational decisions. The result is that some degree of de-regulation, especially for smaller companies, is under way in the 2020s.

Policy matters provide the groundwork for implementation of various rules and procedures within the organization. Appropriate practices in areas such as sexual harassment, diversity and inclusiveness, information security, and code of conduct cannot be systematically infused in the organization unless broad parameters are set in the policy document. The board should regularly review existing policies and, as well, initiate new ones warranted by changes in the business environment or regulation. Cybersecurity, is an example of recently introduced policy in many public companies.

PERFORMANCE

Clearly, a review of some of the filings – especially financial reports – offer an opportunity to the board to examine financial matters, including performance, financial plans, anticipated changes in performance going forward, debt and financial leverage, various risks, and revenue analysis by business segment, customer classification, and geography served. The board may exercise its power to add to its meetings any agenda item on compliance or performance aspects it deems important to explore with management. A candid deliberation with management about why performance is better or worse compared to the guidance (or plan) is important for two reasons: the board would develop insights in drivers of the performance and what could be done to improve the situation, and management would internalize their responsibility to follow up on various aspects of operations that emerged through the dialog with the board. Importantly, besides quarterly and annual reviews of financials, the board may at any time place on the agenda matters related to financial performance or position of the company, often at the time when a major transaction is under consideration, such as a potential acquisition target, entry into a different world region, or funding by issuing additional debt equity.

Allocation of Meeting Time

While the board spends a great deal of time on compliance matters, it should have its eyes on strategy and policy matters. Some might see strategic planning as senior management's responsibility. However, without the board's active engagement in it, results may not be optimal and may perhaps be slow to materialize. If anything, value to the shareholders doesn't come from compliance, but rather from having a sound strategy that is effectively implemented.

The ratio of time devoted to each sphere of accountability – performance and compliance – would vary from meeting to meeting, although time alone is not a good indicator of substantive discussion and sound judgment. The best gauge to assess how balanced the board is in its duties is the board agenda. The board should provide estimated time budgeted for each agenda item, and when addressed in the meeting, it should document any follow up action item(s), the party responsible for it, and a deadline for reporting progress. The agenda should be prepared by the secretary, who may also be the legal counsel of the board. Despite these steps, it is quite possible for a board to slip in its duty toward strategy and policy, for no one outside the board is looking at the board's agendas; the difference due to board inaction on critical matters might not be felt for a while.

To facilitate efficient use of the meeting time, boards may opt to have their own web-based portal, where relevant documents (meeting minutes, agenda, upcoming board resolutions, etc.) can be posted for exclusive and confidential access by the board members. The board members may even vote in advance of the meeting on common resolutions such as the declaration of quarterly dividends, unless there is reason to discuss specific concerns or issues at the meeting.

Finally, any director has the right to call for a closed meeting of independent directors or of the entire board without the presence of management representatives. Such executive sessions, although perhaps not frequent, serve the purpose of an open and candid discussion of key issues among the directors without having to feel constrained by those not on the board. Confidentiality is probably maintained and effective action plans free from management bias are likely to emerge in such sessions.

INTRA-BOARD INTERACTION

Timely, rich, and effective communication among board members, especially at board meetings, is a sign of an active, interested, and progressive board. Three key prerequisites for becoming a board member are: (1) communicate well; (2) respect the law and regulatory compliance; and (3) know the business model of the company you are representing as a board member. There is no substitute for effective communication skills. A board member who does not possess communication skills can be practically considered one less entity in the group for adding value. A deep dive in issues requires that the board member comprehends well the issue on hand. Whereas a legal counsel is available and external expertise can be retained any time, making judgments on issues rests upon the board. As for the company performance, one cannot contribute much to the discussion of strategic, tactical, and operational decisions without knowing well the business model upon which the company is built.

According to a classic article by H. Edward Wrapp in *Harvard Business Review*, the likelihood that one's input will be seriously considered by the group, and may even result in an action plan, is dependent upon the timing of input. Any suggestions in the "corridors of comparative indifference" are likely to be considered seriously, for at this time the group has had enough exposure to the issues and is willing to look at the way in which synergy can be produced. Premature insertion of ideas may go nowhere, for individuals may have staked their determined support for or vehement opposition to the idea. A late injection of suggestions past the corridor of indifference may not result in a change in the outcome, for individuals are likely to have committed to their stand on the issue. In the middle of the scale is an area of comparative indifference where acceptance of a viable solution is highly likely because of the neutrality of those who have not committed to the extremes.

Equally important are other communication skills. Allow sharing of diverse views. When speaking, be brief, precise, and do not use jargon.

Do not be redundant, unless you feel you must emphasize something brought up previously. Understand that time is of the essence and closure of your thoughts is required within a reasonable time. Also, in order not to politicize the issue, try to stay away from personalities; emphasize the issue and processes involved, not people. Be clear, confident, assertive, and convincing in your message. For impact-making input, it would help to mentally rehearse the statements you are about to make.

Finally, while not everyone can sprinkle humor in their conversation, those who can are ahead. A bit of lighter tone in a long, serious dialog injected appropriately could unfreeze colleagues involved in serious thought. It is indeed a talent that can move people by breaking the seriousness a bit.

COMMITTEES OF THE BOARD

While we hear a great deal about the board as a whole, there is very little shared regarding what happens at the committee level. The following paragraphs discuss the proceedings of the board's standing committees.

The Audit Committee

The AC may meet several times in a year, usually on a conference call. However, the committee normally meets in person at least in the same window of time as when the board meets. At such meetings, the committee may discuss the code of conduct, review audit plans with the internal auditors, and discuss reports on controls testing since the last meeting. In most cases, the AC is charged with reviewing reported whistleblower incidents and determining action, if any, to take to address the concern or issue posted by the informant.

The committee also meets with external auditors to comply with formal communication requirements, but more importantly, to learn about any financial matters that the auditors want to share regarding present or anticipated accounting, auditing, or financial reporting developments concerning the company or the industry to which it belongs. Finally, the auditors may have questions for the audit committee; for example, whether the committee or its members are aware of any fraud or misrepresentation. The AC may also ask the external auditors about the work of the internal auditors and their understanding of how well the IAF has performed.

As Warren Buffett suggests, the committee needs to comprehend the work of the independent auditors from the vantage point of different people that "touch" financial statements. Questions like these are important to ask:

- How would the auditors react to the financial statements if they were preparers?

- What questions would the auditors have regarding the financial statements if they were investors?

- How would the auditors react to the statements if they were in the position of the company's CEO? CFO?

The first question allows one to take a look at the issues, challenges, frustrations, or potential errors or omissions the preparer may encounter. This permits a better understanding of the quality of information shared with shareholders. The second question allows the auditors an opportunity to explain how their audit findings and content of financial statements can be conveyed to investors in "plain English," so that the reader can get to substantive questions on financial information. The third question may reveal intricacies of management decisions, such as the choice of an accounting method where alternatives are available and the approach to the development of estimates where such estimates are necessary in financial accounting.

What matters most, however, is an open and candid dialog between the committee and the parties it interacts with. It is essential for the AC to probe emerging financial accounting and reporting questions to a degree where the issue raised and response planned are well understood and responsibility for follow up is assigned.

The Compensation Committee

The compensation committee has at least two major tasks. First, it likely is assigned the responsibility for succession planning. Therefore, using data generated by Human Resources, the committee needs to study the possibilities of a successor for every critical role in the organization.

Questions may arise regarding what is being done to groom such candidates to prepare for stepping into such a role with short notice. Where no viable candidate emerges, the committee needs to identify future actions to correct the situation and who is assigned the accountability for the actions. Second, the compensation committee is charged to determine and propose for a vote the compensation of the chief executive for both the short- and long-term and in cash or other means such as equity (e.g., stock options, restricted stock units) in the company. Typically, every three years, the compensation committee's recommendations, as approved by the board, are put forth to shareholders for an advisory vote.

The Governance Committee

The role of the governance committee extends to providing leadership to the board regarding monitoring and oversight of the board as a group. For example, the committee is responsible for proposing the recruitment of a board member, developing a detailed description of qualification of the board candidate, conducting a search for qualified candidates, and facilitating new board member orientation. The committee also oversees each board member's performance evaluation in addition to the committee evaluations and is answerable for any follow up actions arising from the process. Finally, other matters such as board member training and compensation also could be the responsibility of the governance committee.

Whereas the board in action can be visualized through its proceedings, the bulk of the work that gets done is at the committee level. Of course, each committee is accountable to the board as a whole; accordingly, each must communicate to the board their work and recommendations resulting from it. Hopefully, this leaves more time for the board as a whole to tackle other issues and to have productive dialogs with all parties the board would interact with.

VULNERABILITIES OF THE BOARD

If all that the board does is to cross the t's and dot the i's, it is bound to fail in its duty. Rules, procedures, composition of committees – these are all important, but not the drivers of an effective board. To do well, the board must rise above these threshold requirements of conduct. The board as a body representing shareholders of the company is vulnerable due to many factors, including the following.

Absence of Cohesiveness

If the board members do not represent a unified front, their influence as a body will diminish. Sticking together doesn't mean they have to agree on every point; rather, diversity of opinion and differences in perspectives add to the synergy, although it may seem that it is a disrupter. However, upon closure of an issue, the board as a whole should support the group's decision. Where there is no cohesiveness, individual board members may seek to protect their position, may not fully participate, or react without listening to others' viewpoint. While not every board member may have the knowledge and depth in the issue on hand, it is clear that one needs to engage the best she can on any given issue. Sonnenfeld suggests that well-functioning, successful teams have chemistry that can't be quantified. Such teams seem to get into a virtuous cycle of respect, trust, and candor in which one quality builds on another. For them, equipped with reasonably complete information, a spirited dialog voicing their opinions is the norm rather than an exception.

Halo Effect of Powerful CEOs

Jennings (2006) identifies bigger-than-life CEOs as one of the seven signs of ethical collapse. CEOs and their colleagues in the C-suite can be powerful due to their high impact roles. They wield considerable influence and when they are successful in delivering results, the board may hesitate to question or challenge them. This is even more so when the board chair and the CEO are combined into a single position, and worse yet, the person is also the founder of the company. Ultimately, virtuous behavior while delivering performance is expected, but the disposition of the executive makes him vulnerable to wrongdoing (see Chapter 13). Influential people could "manage" the board agenda to their advantage and recruit people to resort to unauthorized or illegal acts. WorldCom, Satyam Computers, and Madoff's Ponzi scheme thrived because people trusted the person at the helm, without being cautious.

Time and Availability

While many on the outside may see the board role as attending board meetings four or five times in a year, the reality is quite different. Impactful boards are always active; they may not physically meet too often, but members may be called upon to take conference calls frequently. There are other things to do as well, such as flying to Chicago for a day to interview a candidate for external auditor or having dinner with a prospective board member in New York. If a board member is often not available to contribute in this manner, she would be considered ineffective. Availability, therefore, is an important consideration in taking on a board member role. What often causes availability issues is the fact that the board member sits on several boards, dividing the total time available into too many "jobs." Schedule conflicts in such cases become the norm, hampering timely conference calls or travels for board-related tasks. The issue of multiple board membership is a double-edged sword; you want a director with considerable exposure to the world of business and a network of useful contacts. And yet, the value added by a busy board member could be limited because of the time constraints faced by the director. Spencer Stuart, a compensation and human resource consulting firm, analyzed 2018 proxy filings of S&P 500 independent directors and found that 21% of the directors sit on three boards and ten percent serve on four or more boards.

Conflict of Interest

The conflict of interest is inversely related to independence in thought and action. Conflict of interest can crop up in a variety of different contexts, relationships, and incentives. Guarding against existing and potential conflicts of interest is critical to maintaining true independence. Here are a few examples of potential conflicts of interest:

- Representation on company boards where the companies are related in some way, such as a buyer-supplier relationship. Negotiations between the two companies could be colored by self-interest of the board member.

- Dependency on board fees. Once an independent director begins to depend on the remuneration generated from representation on a company board, the behavior of the individual could be biased toward actions that would lead to continuing tenure on the board.

- A variety of other situations or events could cause a compromise in independence. For example, a board member who is currently writing a book hopes to sell enough copies to the company, perhaps one for each employee!

Frailty of Group Dynamics

After all, the board is a group of individuals. As a team, their collective performance could be quite different from what each director can contribute. The synergy of working as a group can be an advantage; however, there are vulnerabilities associated with the group and these could cause the board to do poorly as a group despite individual strengths in play from each director. The side effects of the group dynamics include the tendency toward excessive group conformity and groupthink; bounded rationality and shared information bias; group power, conflict, and polarization.

A form of tendency toward conformity, groupthink is a psychological phenomenon in which people strive for consensus within a group, setting aside their personal conviction. The result is conformity that potentially leads to dysfunctional decision-making. In essence, groupthink results in collapsing the whole board as if there is only one member! Voice of concern and disagreement, spirited discussion and vetting of opposite viewpoints has no room where groupthink prevails. It is believed that groupthink was primarily responsible for some of the issues and fraudulent activities at WorldCom. An antidote for groupthink is a high degree of board cohesiveness.

The board as a group is constrained by bounded rationality, that is, inability to make perfectly rational decisions, and shared information bias. Bounded rationality, both at the individual and group level, points to the incapability to examine all relevant factors to arrive at perfectly rational decisions, thus leading to satisficing rather than optimizing behavior. Shared information bias results from the belief that all information that is relevant and available has been shared, blocking the motivation and creativity to bring in new perspectives, questions, or arguments.

Normally, a board can be considered more equipped to deal with challenges than its directors individually. In this sense, the board can claim to harness the potential synergy from all directors combined. However, this apparent benefit comes with corresponding vulnerabilities of working in a group. The effectiveness of the board can be marginalized by the dynamics of the board. Clearly, a board rich in diversity can be expected to improve monitoring and strategic decision-making. However, the evidence does not uniformly support the expectation that greater board diversity invariably results in better performance.

Some board members could be more influential than others. Some may be more talkative, better communicators, and decidedly more effective in selling their ideas. Age, tenure as a board member, familiarity with industry, board membership elsewhere, and knowledge of the industry to which the company belongs could empower a board member to emphatically express conviction and offer opinions as truths. Presumably, the greater the diversity in the board membership, the greater the likelihood of formation of subgroups within the board along what are called faultlines (hypothetical dividing lines), and the resulting subgroup formation may reduce board effectiveness.

CONDUCT OF THE BOARD CHAIR

An awareness of vulnerabilities of the board is an important first step toward leveraging the board's collective capabilities to the advantage of company performance. A key player who could impact most in addressing such vulnerabilities is the chairman of the board or lead independent director. In the conduct of board meetings, despite timelines and possible lack of time to deal with all issues, the chair has to be tough at times, and flexible at other times. Where an issue is important but ambiguous or ill-defined, it is important to have a dialog without watching the clock; perhaps even a break in the meeting may be appropriate for the directors to reflect on the issues and return with either a reconciliation with the converging viewpoint or conviction of an alternative path.

Executive Sessions

NASDAQ Rule 5605a (2) requires that independent directors must have regularly scheduled meetings at which only independent directors are present, preferably at least twice a year, and maybe more frequently. Known as executive sessions, such meetings are meant to discuss issues that might get a biased treatment due to the presence of powerful non-independent members, including the CEO and perhaps the board chair. Warren Buffett identifies "social difficulty" in the board meetings due to "boardroom atmosphere," which may prevent otherwise intelligent and decent directors from going against the "river's currents." For this reason, Buffett suggests that outside directors must meet without the CEO. The idea is similar, but not identical, to the regulatory definition of executive session, and the purpose is to allow discussion uninfluenced by those who are close to the issue, may even be conflicted, and could sway others toward their biases.

EFFECTIVE BOARDS

Cohesiveness is what binds the group into an effective social unit. Without cohesiveness, the board dynamics would not produce desired results. How does a board foster cohesiveness? In an insightful article in Harvard Business Review, Jeffrey Sonnenfeld explains that a procedural (e.g., tracking board member attendance) or structural (e.g., adding another board committee) change is not the answer to having a thriving board. He suggests that a board is a social group that can be effective only if it acts to build the following within the board: create a climate of trust and candor, foster a culture of open dissent, utilize a fluid portfolio of roles, ensure individual accountability, and evaluate the board's performance.

Transparency is at the root of a climate of trust and candor. Important information should be shared with board members in a timely manner so that members can study and digest the information and raise questions or provide their opinion on related issues. Candor requires uninhibited communication where issues are clearly separated from people. The right to disagree and put forth different solutions, along with its defense, can only be sustained if people in the group trust each other and respect everyone's opinion. Disagreement should be acknowledged as a vital sign of creativity and innovation in problem solving at any level: strategic, tactical, or operational.

Board members need to comprehend the ground realities of running the company operations, and this will not occur systematically unless members are assigned a specific role in a small group where there are opportunities to learn about the realities of running the business and problems that the company faces. In one offshore outsourcing company, the board realized that in spite of having makers and checkers in a transaction data processing chain, errors used to creep in. Some errors were expensive in terms of compensating clients for errors. To study the problem from a high level, it was necessary to form a committee led by a board member with a view to comprehensively understand risks involved and how to mitigate them. One could argue that this is a management issue, not an oversight of management; however, this may be necessary in one-off situations where management needs help in assessing the problem space. After all, there is a thin line between oversight and management and, where appropriate, the board should lean toward helping management without taking away management's accountability.

Independent boards do not necessarily guarantee company performance. To exercise objective judgment driven by one's independence, it is necessary for the board member to have a good understanding of the company, its operations, products, stakeholders, market dynamics, and other environmental factors.

It is apparent that if you value performance in line with clearly identified accountability, you must have a system to collect information that would allow you to evaluate performance in line with the accountability. Without measuring what you are tracking, there would not be any feedback, and as a result, evaluation and follow up. This applies to each board member, board subcommittees, and the board as a whole. A proper identification of the weaknesses and vulnerabilities of each entity (individual, subcommittee, or the board) should help in addressing material weaknesses and thereby improving board performance. To achieve this, a 360 degree performance evaluation is crucial. All evaluations must be reviewed by the governance committee, feedback to individual board members and committees should be provided, and where appropriate, individual board members should be briefed regarding their strengths and weaknesses.

BIBLIOGRAPHY

Buffett, W. 2001. 2001 Chairman's letter. www.berkshirehathaway.com/letters/ 2001pdf.pdf, Accessed October 20, 2019.

Buffett, W. 2002. 2002 Chairman's letter. www.berkshirehathaway.com/letters/ letters.html, Accessed October 20, 2019.

Cadbury, A. 1992. *A Report of The Committee on the Financial Aspects of Corporate Governance (The Cadbury Report)*. London: Gee and Co. Ltd.

Jennings, M. M.. 2006. *The Seven Signs of Ethical Collapse*. New York: St. Martin's Press.

Merchant, K. A. and Pick, K. 2010. *Blind Spots, Biases, and Other Pathologies in the Boardroom*. New York: Business Expert Press.

Peteghem, V. M. and Gaeremynck, L. B. A. 2018. Beyond diversity: A tale of faultlines and frictions in the board of directors. *The Accounting Review* 93 (2): 339–367.

Raval, V. and Godbole, A. 2008. Board portals: are they secure? *JONline*, an electronic journal of ISACA, December 2008, 1–3.

Scharff, M. M. 2005. Understanding WorldCom's accounting fraud: Did group-think play a role?. *Journal of Leadership & Organizational Studies* 11(3): 109–118.

Sonnenfeld, J. A. 2002. What makes great boards great. *Harvard Business Review* September 2002, 106–113.

Spencer Stuart. 2018. *2018 United States Spencer Stuart Board Index*. Chicago: Spencer Stuart.

Wrapp, H. E. 1967. Good managers don't make policy decisions. *Harvard Business Review* September–October, 91–99.

CHAPTER 11

Management and the Board

The relationship between the board and management is unique. The board is exercising oversight on management, while management makes impactful decisions – operational, tactical, and strategic – and implements them. The board is physically remote from the company and its operations; directors spend only a small fraction of time on their governance duties compared to the key executives who dedicate huge amounts of time to the company's operations and strategic direction. Clearly, the board has limited detailed information about the company, its operations, and its performance at granular operational levels. Generally, the board would know only what management would share, except when the board specifically asks for particular information; therefore, there exists information asymmetry between the two. This is not for lack of interest on the part of board members to learn about the company's operations; the fact is that without hands-on exposure to the operations, it simply is not possible to fully soak up the realities of the company's ins and outs.

Both the board and senior management are powerful groups, each with its own leverage. The board can fire the CEO, or the CEO may leave if unsatisfied, for example, with how the board deals with management. Overall, significant influence seems to rest on management's side. And yet, management likely recognizes that it cannot survive without a healthy relationship with the board.

WHO "CONTROLS" WHOM?

It would be simplistic to assume that the board "controls" the CEO. In fact, CEOs wield considerable influence, call their own shots, and passionately drive the company they lead. Successful CEOs are typically aggressive, demanding results from their managers, and keeping managers focused on the company's performance. Add to this measure of influence additional boost from the equity ownership by the CEO personally, or by the CEO's family, and their foundation(s). Take, for example, Tesla Corporation and its CEO, Elon Musk. As a visionary leader, he has carved out for himself a role that is not separate from the destiny of Tesla. He also owns a substantial number of outstanding shares. Although he does not own a majority of voting shares, his stake in the company is enough to approve or block key changes in the company. This is because the company's bylaws require a supermajority vote (two-thirds of votes) for approval of any resolutions, including shareholder proposals. This adds up to almost unchallenged control of the company, leaving him to exercise influence in his own way. In 2019, he surprised the investor community by tweeting, without the board's knowledge, that he would take the company private and had secured the funding to do so. Tweeting as a communication channel has not been recognized to reach the shareholders wholly and uniformly. Also, the decision to go private is a board prerogative; no single shareholder can usurp the board prerogative. The SEC followed up and settled with Mr. Musk, who agreed to pay a fine, step down as chair of the company's board, and committed to oversight of his public statements. Subsequently, Mr. Musk violated the oversight by tweeting a message, and the matter was once again addressed by the SEC. It may not be surprising if shareholders of Tesla perceive the board as not really independent of the company's CEO.

Balancing Competing Powers

The question is not who controls whom; rather, the challenge is in balancing the influence of two powerful forces, the board and management, to create long-term value for shareholders. The overriding intent should be to develop shared expectations between the board and management and for each to work toward them in their unique roles. Management is ultimately responsible for the company performance, and the board exists to control and direct management. It is the board's duty to support, guide, and counsel management where necessary. The oversight role thus is not in the spirit of sitting on the sideline and watching the "game." Some degree of intervention on the part of the board may be appropriate and may even be necessary for management to continue to achieve targets developed and committed. Neither the board nor management should trip on the other's turf while working on shared expectations. Where the board decidedly intrudes on management's turf, it should be clear that it is doing so only to assist management and at the implicit invitation of management to do so. All such intrusions should be limited and properly scoped so the withdrawal by the board from such activity can be clearly signaled.

An example of board intrusion should clarify the discussion above. An offshore outsourcing company was planning to launch a new line of services in ERP (Enterprise Resource Planning) for its customers. However, the internal knowhow on this rather complex field was limited; consequently, the company was struggling to develop an ERP-based system for its use. It did not make sense to pitch a service to the company's customers if some degree of internal use was not demonstrated. The commitment was lacking, employee motivation was low, and users were distinctly against an internal ERP system because they felt it was likely to fail. ERP developers were few and in high demand in the job market, making the recruitment of experienced people less fruitful. To resolve the dilemma, the board was asked to intervene. After a daylong meeting of prospective users and developers with one of the board members, it was agreed that the developers would try to generate internal knowledge about ERP systems if external experts were engaged as consultants for a few months. The board supported the idea and the project was back on track. Ultimately, the ERP practice grew at a healthy pace.

Aligning Senior Management Accountability

It is important to align the board's responsibility to direct and provide oversight on management's responsibility to plan and deliver performance, both in the short- and long-run. Table 11.1 summarizes the relationship between common senior management responsibilities with the board oversight function. Item A clearly belongs to the board. This is the single most critical duty of the board. If the right CEO is appointed, the rest of the governance becomes a little easier. Without a competent

TABLE 11.1 Relationship between common senior management functions and the board oversight

	Senior management		The board
A			Recruit CEO and senior managers. Develop and review succession plans for senior management.
B	Develop corporate strategy.		Approve corporate strategy.
C	Risk management.		Ensure that risks are aligned with risk appetite. Oversee senior manager designated as responsible for risk management.
D	Set the tone-at-the-top.		Approve and monitor tone-at-the-top.
E	Implement strategy.		Monitor strategy implementation.
F	Produce financial statements. Make timely and transparent disclosures.	Work with auditors in obtaining assurance on financial statements.	Discuss and monitor financial performance and compliance with financial reporting. Provide liaison with the auditors.
G	Develop and implement business resiliency and crisis management plan.		Provide oversight on business resiliency plan.
H	Shareholder engagement.		Shareholder engagement.

person of high integrity at the helm, there is more to do on the part of the board, and yet, results may not be as expected. Items B, C, and D belong to management, but not without close oversight from the board. Item E flows from Item B and is the responsibility of management. Item F describes normal duties of the senior management team and Item G is owned by management. None of these are left completely to management; the board wants to provide effective oversight on each of the items, from B to G. The final item, H, is a joint responsibility of management and the board, where management mostly communicates issues of operations, strategy, and financial results, while the board answers questions of governance, parlays with activist shareholders (see Chapter 12) and grapples with shareholder proposals. Shareholder communication with senior management is often structured (quarterly conference calls, for example); the board more than likely communicates using unstructured means, such as face-to-face meetings or correspondence with shareholders, including institutional investors.

Compliance versus Performance

A microscopic look at the board agenda should tell you that the board invests a substantial amount of time in its regulatory compliance oversight duty relative to management performance monitoring. If there is no compliance, chances are, the company will run into trouble and the board may be held accountable. Without compliance, the company's reputation and therefore, the future may be at stake. In contrast, there are few instances where the board was held responsible for poor performance or unwise investments by management. Despite best intentions, management may run into failed decisions which cost the company money and may cause a drag on the company's performance for some time. The board may review and approve, or disapprove, all investments proposed by management above a preestablished threshold amount and "in sync" with the company's strategic plan. However, this may not necessarily result in optimal company performance. Often, company performance issues and the CEO's competency to drive results come through shareholder proposals or activism by influential investors if the board fails to correct the situation in a timely manner.

The broad generalization above needs to be moderated by the argument that every case is different. There are startups and there are mature companies; there are companies that grow well organically, requiring very little expansion through acquisitions. The German company Aldi serves as an example of impressive organic growth. Depending on the company's stage in life, it may be that the board pays more attention to company performance. The board's focus on company performance could be significant just prior to the launch of IPO; however, at this time, it is also necessary to take a close look at conflicts of interest (e.g., the company loan to the CEO is not permitted in a public company). We Company considered an IPO, but failed for some reasons, including (1) growth of revenue accompanied by massive losses, and (2) related party involvement in the operations (Rebekah Neumann as an executive) and transactions (leasing the CEO properties for the company business) of the company.

When a new CEO takes charge, the board may want to deliberately put more time in coaching the CEO, especially if the candidate is recruited from outside. Also, proposals regarding a possible merger or acquisition should be reviewed and endorsed (or rejected) by the board. Without the board's approval, transactions involving significant investments or high risks may not be conducted by management.

An interesting pattern that emerges from regulatory requirements is that they predominantly address compliance, not performance. It is, indeed, challenging if not impossible for the regulators to direct what the company's management should do to achieve the desired performance; they can only provide parameters for how it should conduct itself within the context of shareholders and the board. This is one reason why there are no best practices or guidelines offered by the SEC regarding, say, strategic planning. OECD or NACD offer such advice only as a resource, not a requirement.

MANAGEMENT'S LEGAL DUTY

Until the enactment of SOX, a clear delineation of what management is responsible for was not available, although some of the signed assertions were part of the internal document, for example, signed CFO certification submitted to the auditor. Rather, the focus in the past was on the board and the auditors. This changed greatly as SOX explicitly identified what management is responsible for in the matter of governance. Figure 11.1 presents key areas of management accountability. To summarize:

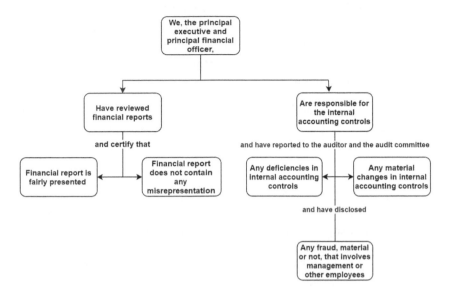

FIGURE 11.1 Management's responsibility for financial reports and internal accounting controls.

- To dissolve ambiguity between the role of the auditor and management, SOX clarified that the financial statements audited by the independent auditors are the responsibility of management; they are in all respects the preparers of the financial information and therefore accountable with respect to truthfulness of the information shared.

- Since the reliability of the financial information hinges upon the adequacy and effectiveness of internal controls, SOX required management to "own" the internal control framework, test it regularly, and certify if it has any significant deficiencies or material weaknesses. In this regard, the external auditors are required to provide an opinion on the assessment of internal controls by management. Table 11.2 provides additional information regarding ICFR and management's responsibility.

- Both the CEO and the CFO are required to certify that (1) (quarterly and annual) reports are accurate and complete; (2)

adequate internal controls over financial reporting (ICFR) have been established and maintained; and (3) deficiencies in, and changes to, internal accounting controls have been reported. Arguably, this may nurture greater confidence in the accuracy, quality, and reliability of a company's reports.

- To provide "teeth" to the law, the lawmakers included stiff penalties and the possibility of criminal investigation followed by severe punishments where appropriate.

TABLE 11.2 ICFR and the management's responsibility

Strong internal controls over financial reporting (ICFR) provide a degree of confidence in the veracity of the company's financial statements. Viewed in this manner, ICFR is a prerequisite to reliable financial information. Management is responsible for establishing and maintaining adequate ICFR. For evaluating effectiveness of ICFR, management should use a framework, such as the COSO framework. Based on the management's evaluation of ICFR, it should report its conclusions about effectiveness of ICFR.

As a result of its evaluation of ICFR, management may find control deficiencies. A control deficiency exists when the design or operation of a control does not allow management or employees, in the normal course of performing their assigned functions, to prevent or detect misstatements on a timely basis (PCAOB, AS 1305). Normally, the lack of effectiveness of internal controls is identified in increasing levels of severity as control deficiency, significant deficiency, or material weakness. A significant deficiency, or a combination of deficiencies, in ICFR suggests levels of severity enough to merit attention by those responsible for oversight of the company's financial reporting. A material weakness is a significant deficiency, or a combination of significant deficiencies, such that there is a reasonable possibility that a material misstatement of the company's financial statements will not be prevented or detected on a timely basis. Any material weakness is rated as posing a higher risk than an isolated significant deficiency in internal controls.

In its annual internal control report, management must (1) state that it is the responsibility of the management for establishing and maintaining an adequate internal control structure and procedures for financial reporting and (2) provide an assessment of the internal control structure and procedures of the company for financial reporting. Finally, ICFR includes disclosure controls to ensure that all required disclosures are made accurately and completely.

STRATEGIC PLANNING

A strategic plan probably is the most fundamental document agreed upon by the chief executive and his leadership team to pursue in achieving the long-term company goals. The strategic plan forms the basis for company operations and drives performance in the long run. As such, the plan is owned by management with full accountability; however, the board cannot leave management alone, it must review the plan preferably while in formation, and probe or guide management in arriving at a realistic, challenging but achievable set of goals consistent with the company's risk appetite. In the process, one expected outcome is that the board would have influenced strategic thinking, innovation, and entrepreneurship skills. Besides, a management-board dialog could result in internal validation of the plan and a degree of comfort to the executives due to support from the board.

One might wonder why, if ever, the board should interfere with the planning process undertaken by management. The reason is that the board is responsible for oversight on the company performance and this is unlikely to be delivered unless it strives to understand and "bless" the plan. Besides, there might be specific circumstances that call for some degree of board intervention. For example, a highly successful manager of outsourcing services in the financial services sector was promoted to the position of CEO. An otherwise perfectly capable executive, his tendencies were more like problem-solving in his area of work, and he was exceptionally successful in doing so. However, as CEO, he needed to become comfortable with the organization-wide planning process. The board coached the CEO and supported him during the planning process in his first year at the helm. He became quite successful as the CEO. Without the board intervention in the first year of planning, this would not have happened.

Even the seasoned CEOs have their biases, which may push them to shirk certain types of risky adventures. A CEO of a company with revenue over $500 million had once tried to acquire and integrate a small company, but had failed miserably. The experience translated into a complete burnout from growth by acquisition. He needed help in understanding the key arguments in favor of acquisitions, the role of acquisitions in company growth, and risk-based due diligence in the acquisition process. If the board accepted this phobia and did not intervene to help the CEO, it could presumably limit the potential performance of the company.

Any plan, even an annual budget, has a better chance of materializing if the managers responsible for it own the process and are engaged in the development of goals. Without management's participation, the plan probably will not get a chance of dedicated and utmost effort on the part of executives to deliver the milestones in the plan. Consequently, it is important for the board to not directly intrude, but rather help validate the assumptions behind the plan, help improve the planning process, ensure that an appropriate amount of resources are committed to the plan, and verify that risks implicit in the plan are consistent with expectations.

Annual Budgets

Strategic plans cover the long term, say, five to ten years, while annual budgets are for one-year term, sometimes prepared on a rolling 12-month or four-quarter cycle. Annual budgets are not standalone products; in part, they are derived from or at least contingent upon the company's strategic plan. Thus, annual budgets are nested in the strategic plan and success of the plan determines at least partially how well the budgets are attained.

Management's guidance regarding quarterly and annual revenues and earnings is likely based on the budgets. Because the market punishes companies that underperform compared to the guidance, it is very important for management to set, and for the board to understand, the guidance figures and how they were determined. It is important for the CEO and CFO to be transparent and timely about any changes that they expect from the previously delivered guidance. Incidentally, because numerous companies offer earnings guidance, there is the assumption that providing such guidance is a requirement. The truth is, companies are not required to offer guidance to investors. However, most companies are followers rather than leaders, they cannot afford to have investors and shareholders make assumptions about earnings and revenue, for this may cause a considerable expectation gap and consequent undue volatility in the market price of the company's shares. Some companies follow the middle path. They provide basic projections (revenue and gross margins, for example) and leave the forecasting of earnings in the hands of the shareholders, analysts, and prospective investors.

MONITORING PERFORMANCE

Monitoring management's performance is clearly an important board duty. After all, shareholders put a great deal of weight on how the company is doing financially, for growth of their investment value and returns depend on it. The board should periodically review management's performance relative to the targets set through the planning process.

Most companies have an integrated dashboard of measures that they track on a regular basis. These include both financial and non-financial measures, and some of these may be a part of the formula for determining compensation of key executives. If the measures include both historic performance and leading indicators, collectively, such a scorecard would be considerably helpful in monitoring the company's performance.

Performance Measurement Metric: An Example

One widely known strategic measurement and management system, called the Balanced Scorecard (BSC), was developed by Drs. Robert Kaplan and David Norton. Their work emerged from the challenge to connect in a holistic manner short-term goals and objectives to long-term plans. According to them, in an ever-changing, competitive, and highly interconnected environment, a firm can no longer rely on the traditional approach of solely focusing on financial measures that mask the relationship of such measures to value-creating non-financial measures. Traditional models suffer from the lack of an explicit identification of the linkage between long-term strategies of a company, formulated mostly by top management, and the short-term operational measures, which are often in the form of budgets. This deficiency limits management's potential to drive performance and is often the reason for failure of many organizations in executing strategy effectively.

The BSC has the potential to improve firm performance for various reasons. It offers a holistic, disciplined approach to measuring and managing an entity's progress toward its mission, goals, and objectives.

In addition to commitment of the firm's leadership, it requires involvement of the entire hierarchy. Because of the presence of the BSC, stakeholders are aware of the organization's vision and path to achieve it. The organization is fully and constantly involved in measuring and monitoring progress toward goals, identifying which parts of the value chain need improvement, and allocating resources with a focus on improvement of processes and people skills to bridge such deficiencies.

As Kaplan and Norton state, the BSC is a comprehensive framework that translates a company's strategic objectives into a coherent set of performance measures. To extend the financial perspective, the BSC typically adds three complementary, non-financial perspectives: customer, internal business processes, and innovation and learning. The customer perspective focuses on the satisfaction of the firm's customer base and how well their expectations are being met. Supplementing the customer perspective is the internal business perspective, which takes into consideration the business processes that have a significant impact on the company's value chain and aims at bettering these processes. The innovation and learning perspective emphasizes continual improvement to existing products and processes and the ability to introduce entirely new products with expanded capabilities. As with the traditional method, the financial perspective examines bottom line numbers such as return on investment, return on equity, operating income, and cash flow. Importantly, the scorecard makes explicit the relationships between such financial measures (lagging indicators) with measures in the other three non-financial perspectives (leading indicators). This in turn provides insights on how to drive performance by leveraging these relationships.

Whereas the BSC is relatively more known, its implementation is resource- and time-intensive. There are several other dashboard models available which may suit the firm wishing to put in place a good metric. Often, the firms would create their own customized dashboard. In any case, it is best for the board and management to have a holistic metric that is consistent with its strategy and budgets, so that progress can be tracked and variances from expectations can be investigated and addressed.

From a comprehensive dashboard throwing much light on cause and effect between financial results and non-financial drivers, the shareholders may get to view mainly the measures within the financial perspective. Occasionally, in its explanation of the reported financial results, management may use non-financial measures, such as the backlog of sales orders in terms of number of months of plant capacity utilization.

Non-GAAP Measures

Management often communicates information that is not in compliance with Generally Accepted Accounting Principles (GAAP). Such measures are called non-GAAP measures. Examples include breakouts of segments and margins, detailed analysis of revenues, and EBITDA (Earnings Before Interest, Taxes, Depreciation, and Amortization). Management reports such measures outside of the audited or reviewed financial statements, for example, in the Management Discussion & Analysis (MD&A) segment in the annual report or in the earnings release. The presentation of many non-GAAP measures begins with a GAAP-reported figure from the audited or reviewed financial statements.

Non-GAAP measures are used not because GAAP-based measures are deficient; rather, the purpose is to provide additional information that may be helpful to the user. A variety of reasons promote the use of non-GAAP measures. Such measures may provide granular business segment information, improving transparency. Non-financial non-GAAP measures, such as the number of website clicks, may be helpful to the user of financial statements. In some cases, they may exclude effects of certain unique transactions or extraordinary or non-recurring items that could presumably distort the financials. In this regard, the defense for reporting such measures is that comparability of data over time is improved. Additionally, there might be rare areas where GAAP is an indication of deficiency and a non-GAAP measure corrects this void. Once started, it might be difficult for companies to stop reporting such non-GAAP measures, for the users might consider their absence as a red flag.

Normally, the SEC discourages the use of non-GAAP measures, for the user may not be able to (1) reconcile such measures with other measures for the same company or (2) compare such measures across companies, perhaps because other companies do not report these non-GAAP measures. The use of non-GAAP measures may be rejected on the grounds that they presumably create bias and perhaps confusion due to a non-standard approach to their calculation. At times, it is alleged that management reports non-GAAP measures only when they want the performance to look good, compared to the GAAP-based performance. This may be the case particularly at a time when a startup is ready to issue the IPO. For example, the Wall Street Journal reported in 2019 that Lyft, We Company, and Peloton Interactive used different measures to suggest profitability of the company. Lyft used adjusted EBITDA and "contribution" (Revenue minus direct expenses) to show that it has promising future, while the audited net income has been a net loss since its inception in 2012. We Company recognized in its IPO filing that it may be unable to achieve profitability at a company level, but delivered an optimistic opinion by declaring that it generated positive contribution margin (revenue minus direct expenses) at the business unit level. And Peloton emphasized that its gross profit was positive, although the bottom line never turned black from the initial launch through the issue of its IPO. Warren Buffett, CEO of Berkshire Hathaway, sums it up well in his 2002 letter to the shareholders: proforma earnings, a non-GAAP measure, is a means for managers to invariably show "earnings" far in excess of those allowed by their auditors.

Non-GAAP measures are often unique to the company or the industry to which it belongs. For example, the oil exploration firms report the present value of crude oil reserves over a period of ten years at a discount rate of ten percent. Such measures are hard to fold into the required GAAP-based metric. At a minimum, the firm should include a definition of the non-GAAP measure reported, and the users should be careful in interpreting such measures. Internal controls over non-GAAP measures do not necessarily alleviate the concern that such measures are subject to interpretation and even manipulation. Internally, the directors should ensure that non-GAAP measures, if included in the executive compensation formula, will not generate dysfunctional behavior on the part of management. Perhaps it is best to avoid any non-GAAP measures in the measurement of executive compensation.

Performance-Related Oversight

There are several areas that could become part of the firm's strategy and yet are a concern for the board of directors. Major financing decisions would fall in this category. If management develops a strategy to restructure debt or increase debt leverage, the board would be interested in knowing the detailed plans and may even insist on the board approval of the plan. Or if management plans to acquire another business at a certain price, the board would have significant input and, depending on the relative size of investment, may insist on a board vote for approval of the transaction. As such, any future action that would directly impact shareholder returns and risks would come under the board's microscope. For example, share buyback would shrink the number of shares outstanding and therefore increase earnings per share even when the earnings remain flat year over year. Therefore, funds allocated for share buyback are subject to board approval. Primarily as a tax planning exercise, companies also consider whether to keep the USA as the domicile or go offshore to save on taxes. Such tax planning moves are important strategic actions for management's consideration. Because these will have direct and potentially significant impact on shareholder risk and returns, the board intervention in the decision is expected.

At a minimum, in strategic planning, a clear "line in the sand" is difficult to draw defining the board role versus that of management. At times, both will have to live with a degree of closeness and disregard intervention in each other's turf as a non-issue, at least for the specific situation under consideration.

EXECUTIVE COMPENSATION

Rewards comprise a strong, if not the only, reason performance is delivered in the world of business. A strong motivation to work toward an organization's goals is therefore the expectation that rewards will follow upon achievement of the goals. The CEO and his top team are no different; they, too, are incentivized by the rewards they expect. Therefore, the alignment of CEO compensation with the firm's performance is central to effective governance. Setting this instrumentality within the compensation formula is the key challenge for the board and its compensation committee.

The link between motivation for performance and reward has been investigated for decades. Notable among the many theories of motivation is Porter and Lawler's theory of managerial motivation and performance. Derived from Victor Vroom's expectancy theory, it offers a more complete normative explanation of the relationship between performance and rewards, moderated by various factors including perceived fairness of rewards, nature of rewards (extrinsic or intrinsic), and task requirements and ability to achieve the task. In the corporate governance arena, the debate rages around whether the alignment between the CEO's performance and his compensation is optimal in motivating the chief executive to deliver set goals. Many argue that executive compensation and company performance are not ideally linked, and for various reasons, could be severely out of alignment. The issue often results in shareholder proposals to better address the alignment.

Role of Compensation Consultants

Normally, the board approves both the short-term and long-term executive compensation plan and asks shareholders to provide a nonbinding vote on the plan, a step that is called Say-on-Pay (SOP). Clearly, shareholder disapproval of the plan could result in a significant fallout with some time lag, if not immediately. The board therefore would like to propose a plan that is acceptable to a large majority of the voting shareholders, even though the vote as such is nonbinding.

To achieve this objective, the board likely would engage a compensation consulting firm to advise on the construction of the plan. Typically, the manager of human resources would be involved in seeking a competent consultant, although it is the board that hires the consultant. To have a compensation consultant advise the board is not required, but it certainly helps the board get a degree of comfort around the plan and, as well, may project a perception of thorough work in developing the plan. It is conceivable that boards with limited experience in executive compensation and little access to the peer group compensation data would prefer to hire a consultant, at least in initial years, to mitigate any risk of misalignment between the CEO's performance and compensation.

Shareholder Say-on-Pay (SOP)

The board's oversight extends to the setting of management's compensation, especially the CEO's compensation. Companies should design properly aligned executive compensation plans to avoid having to restructure payments after receiving a low level of SOP support. Unfavorable SOP outcomes might have undesirable consequences for the firm, including negative publicity, the exit of competent top executives, and costs of changes in the compensation packages.

It is the board's duty to develop executive compensation plans and see that the compensation is judged as fair by the executives involved and also meet with shareholder expectations expressed in a nonbinding vote of the shareholders. Normally recognized as Say-on-Pay (SOP), this regulatory requirement in the USA presumably provides for greater compensation transparency in communication with the shareholders.

In theory, the SOP requirement is an anomaly. The more involved the principal (shareholders) in a firm's managerial decisions, the more difficult it is for the directors (agents) to be held accountable for the outcomes of those decisions. If the board is exercising oversight, shouldn't the shareholders also leave the matters of CEO compensation to the board? Perhaps the regulators believe that this in an important instrumentality between the company's performance and the CEO's rewards and therefore requires a special consideration. In accordance with the requirement, the board submits an executive compensation plan for a shareholder vote at the annual general meeting of the company. The shareholders may vote in person at the meeting, although most exercise their choice through the proxy vote.

The outcome of the shareholder vote, although nonbinding, has significant consequences. The board certainly would hope that an over-whelming majority of shareholders would vote in favor of the plan put forth by the board. However, there are reasons to believe that this may not occur. For example, shareholders are constrained by information asymmetry; they may not have all the information necessary to make an informed judgment. Secondly, even if they have necessary information, they may not be familiar with the compensation issues, challenges of managerial motivation, or how to determine a satisfactory plan that would motivate management to take on a challenging but achievable goal. To illustrate, what does it take to improve the returns from a negative 9% to a negative 4% in a year? Would that 5% improvement take the same effort as a jump from a positive 3% to a positive 8% return? Additionally, what strategic actions would come into play in moving the needle higher, and what are the risks associated with these actions? Answers to these and other questions are important, but most individual shareholders may not have either the requisite knowledge or the decision model to judge if the proposed compensation is fair in relation to the expected performance.

Because of these limitations, the result of the vote may produce more noise than clarity on the choices reflected in the plan. The board, of course, would like to see that an overwhelming majority of the shareholders would approve of the plan, but when this does not happen, what should the board do? In the period immediately following results of the vote, there may not be room for a quick change. However, the board would likely consider shareholder opinion in setting compensation in future. It is important to note that the CEO also has the right to consider the shareholder vote in her decision to stay or leave the company. A significant degree of disapproval may simply lead the CEO to conclude that the board has lost trust of the shareholders or it is not perceived as independent from management.

Often, the alarming fact is the size of the compensation. Executive compensation in absolute terms has skyrocketed. At issue is the question: does the CEO deserve such outsize compensation? Apparently, there is a great deal of hesitation among some shareholders that the top executive does not merit such rewards. Adding to this confusion is the required disclosure of the ratio of the executive compensation to the mean salary of employees in the same company. Value judgments arising from such information are often biased against the CEO. There does not appear to be any conceptually sound argument regarding what the benchmark ratio should be.

Finally, the challenges of executive compensation vary with the specific situation of the company. For example, the issue of executive compensation may be mute in owner-managed companies where the owner controls a majority of voting shares. To avoid conflict with other shareholders, the owner may take a token salary of, say, $100,000 and no bonuses for superior performance. A low level of SOP shareholder support is unlikely in this case, however, if it happens, the board will have to do a lot more thinking!

Other Compensation Issues

Share Buyback

If the company is engaging in share buyback, the result would be an increase in the earnings per share. However, this is only because the number of shares issued and outstanding (the denominator in the ratio) has decreased and not because the earnings (the numerator) as such have increased. The board, in developing its executive compensation formula, must clearly identify how the effect of share buyback on financials will be treated. Theoretically, management should not get credit for improvement in earnings per share on account of share buyback.

Golden Parachute

An agreement between a company and its senior management (such as the CEO), a golden parachute identifies specific benefits (cash bonus, stock options, etc.) that would accrue to the executive in the event of termination of employment resulting from mergers or takeovers. The agreement protects valuable top executives from the loss of a job on account of change in control.

Incentives and Behavior

Humans are tempted to indulge, in the process they compromise their moral resolution. Such acts may result in financial fraud. Therefore, it is important to recognize that incentives could make people lose self-control and volitionally act in their self-interest. Organizational wrong-doing is an ongoing phenomenon and is unlikely to be eradicated. In setting executive compensation, it is important to consider if the incentives are loaded to encourage indulgence. An example here should prove helpful. Several decades ago, a Fortune 500 company set the executive compensation on the basis of cash flow. The executive noticed there would be a shortfall in the goal, so he deferred a key capital investment project and thus met the cash flow requirement!

Clawback

A clawback provision in an executive compensation plan signifies potential recovery of forfeited incentives (e.g., bonuses). For example, if incentives were paid to the executives who had manipulated financial numbers or committed fraud, upon knowing about the wrongdoing, the company recovers the incentives paid to the executive. This is one way to create an obstacle to executive fraud.

CONFLICTS AND CHALLENGES

Top executives are powerful influencers; they persist to produce results. Without strong and competent senior management at the helm, prospects for shareholder returns are limited, at best. Professional management is the key to the company's long-term growth in the best interests of investors.

The tremendous advantage of trusting professional management to run the company comes with its own risks. After all, executives are human and, like everyone else, they could fall prey to moral temptations. As discussed in Chapter 13, this is especially true of a large majority of executives that exhibit high narcissistic tendencies. Narcissism has many traits, some of which could prompt aggressive self-interested behavior at the cost of the company's stakeholders. The result could be that top management strengths could give way to a major corporate meltdown if and when the self-interests take priority over the fiduciary duty to shareholders.

Most investors want quick results; they are not satisfied with prospective long-term promises. Earnings guidance and the company's financial performance relative to the guidance is important to them. This in turn causes what is called short-termism, a managerial tendency to make things look good in the near term, even if the decision is not desirable from a long-term perspective. Managerial behavior that emphasizes short-term results, also described as managerial myopia, could result in suboptimal long-term returns to the shareholders. There is a risk that the executive compensation formula adopted by the company stresses near-term performance, in which case the risk that management would cut corners to produce immediate positive returns is high. Harnessing the powerful force of executives in the best interests of the stakeholders is a delicate exercise.

BIBLIOGRAPHY

Armstrong, C. S., Ittner, C. D. and Larcker, D. F. 2012. Corporate governance, compensation consultants, and CEO pay levels. *Review of Accounting Studies* 17(2): 322–351.

Buffett, W. 2002. 2002 Chairman's letter, www.berkshirehathaway.com/letters/letters.html, Accessed October 20, 2019.

de Kluyver, C. A. 2009. *A Primer on Corporate Governance*. New York: Business Expert Press.

Eaglesham, J. 2019. Tech firms' profit claims draw scrutiny. *The Wall Street Journal*, September 23, B4.

Kaplan, R. S. and Norton, D. P. 1992. The balanced scorecard: Measures that drive performance. *Harvard Business Review* 70(1): 71–79.

Kaplan, R. S. and Norton, D. P. 1993. Putting the balanced scorecard to work. *Harvard Business Review* 71(5): 134–147.

Kaplan, R. S. and Norton, D. P. 1996a. *Translating Strategy into Action: the Balanced Scorecard*. Boston, MA: Harvard Business School Publishing Corporation.

Kaplan, R. S. and Norton, D. P. 1996b. Using the balanced scorecard as a strategic management system. *Harvard Business Review* July–August, 2007 85(7–8): 150–161.

Kaplan, R. S. and Norton, D. P. 2001a. Transforming the balanced scorecard from performance measurement to strategic management: Part I. *Accounting Horizons* 15(1): 87–104.

Kaplan, R. S. and Norton, D. P. 2001b. Transforming the balanced scorecard from performance measurement to strategic management: Part II. *Accounting Horizons* 15(2): 147–160.

Kaplan, R. S. and Norton, D. P. 2001c. *The Strategy-Focused Organization: how Balanced Scorecard Companies Thrive in the New Business Environment*. Boston, MA: Harvard Business School Publishing Corporation.

Porter, L. W. and Lawler, E. E. 1968. *Managerial Attitudes and Performance*. Homewood, IL: Richard D. Irwin.

Sanchez-Marin, G., Lozano-Reina, G. and Baixauli-Soler, J. S. 2017. Say on pay effectiveness, corporate governance mechanisms, and CEO compensation alignment. *Business Research Quarterly* 20: 226–239.

Wingender, J. R., Jr., Raval, V. and Schuett, S. J. 2015. The impact of balanced scorecard hall of fame induction announcement on firm value. *International Journal of Economic Behavior* 5: 121–132.

Wongrassamee, S., Gardiner, P. D. and Simmons, J. E. L. 2003. Performance measurement tools: The balanced scorecard and the EFQM excellence model. *Measuring Business Excellence* 7(1): 14–29.

CHAPTER 12

Shareholder Communication and Engagement

The inevitable separation of ownership from management causes benefits and downsides. A benefit is that a number of entities, including individuals, can participate in the ownership of the company. But this comes at the cost of not having access to the company's information system, including information relevant to shareholder decision-making (e.g., buy, hold, or sell shares) with respect to their investment in the company. Shareholders suffer from information asymmetry: the management has all the data and the shareholders get largely structured, summarized information periodically. An exception might be triggered when the company is required to report an incident or an issue to the shareholders in real time. For example, if the board receives a whistleblower report suggesting that the CEO's behavior is unethical, the shareholders would need to know as soon as possible without waiting for the next reporting cycle. This is communicated by filing with the SEC an appropriate form (e.g., Form 6-k for foreign companies with ADRs listed on a U.S. stock exchange).

To deal with the rights of shareholders to receive information and express their voice on key matters of the company, most countries enact laws. A primary purpose is to protect the rights of the shareholders and at the same time, to prohibit anyone with access to critical and timely

TABLE 12.1 Insider trading

Well-known homemaking celebrity Martha Stewart had invested in securities of ImClone, a biopharmaceutical company. In 2001, her stockbroker called to convey that the U.S. Food and Drug Administration has rejected ImClone's new cancer drug and as a result, the company's share price would fall sharply once the information was made public. Ahead of the negative news, she sold securities at a gain, trading on the insider information.

In another case, Rajat Gupta, former Goldman Sachs board member and retired head of McKinsey & Co., allegedly shared information with a fund manager, Raj Rajaratnam, about Berkshire Hathaway's decision to invest in Goldman Sachs. Gupta was convicted of illegally sharing insider information.

information from taking advantage of it for personal gain. Abuse of information that is material and time-sensitive, not yet disclosed publicly, and relevant to valuation of shares often results in insider trading, that is, buying or selling the securities of the company by an individual or his or her relatives on the basis of relevant information not yet made public. Table 12.1 discusses and illustrates insider trading.

ATTRIBUTES OF INFORMATION

Information that senior management shares with shareholders should be communicated efficiently with the attempt to reach all who have presumed interest in such information. Communicating with a segment or group of investors any new information may result in improper or inadequate communication. The medium chosen should be commonly used by those who have an interest in receiving such information. The most reliable way to attempt to reach every shareholder is by filing the information with the SEC. If Twitter is not likely to reach all shareholders, its use could compromise the intention of equitable and immediate distribution to everyone entitled to receive the information. The SEC pursued Elon Musk, who had attempted to tweet a message suggesting that he planned to take Tesla Motors private. The content in the message was not approved by the board, nor was there a formal proposal to take the company private. Mr. Musk settled with the SEC and agreed to be discrete about the use of Tweeter in shareholder communication.

Asymmetry

There is clearly a big difference between (1) what management knows and (2) what the shareholders know about the company's near-term destiny and long-term outlook. This is because management is running the operations and setting and executing the company's tactical and strategic plans. The board as shareholders' agent is more likely well informed about the company's ongoings and yet, perhaps may not be as well informed as management would be. Practically, management, the board members, and other coregulators such as the independent auditors are "insiders" while the remaining shareholders are "outsiders." There clearly is an information asymmetry between insiders and outsiders, that is, some insiders and others associated with governance may know more, at least for a time, than the shareholders at large. As discussed previously, the abuse of privileged information, while it is still not in the hands of shareholders, is considered a violation, such as the insider trading.

Some, if not all, of the asymmetry could result with insiders having an edge over the outsiders in predicting, for example, the company's share price. An insider could gain, often at the cost of the outsiders, in trading the securities of the company prior to the time the information becomes public. For example, the company may be looking into a buyout offer from another firm at a certain price per share. Those involved in due diligence of such an offer are privileged and may use the information to trade, or prompt someone to trade, in the shares of the company to their advantage. To prevent insiders from gaining unfair advantage from the heretofore undisclosed information, regulations prohibit trading of shares by the insiders throughout the window of time during which information relevant to the investment decision is not made public, possibly eliminating the effect of asymmetry. Any violation of such rules is punished, making the trade far less attractive to the insider.

In publicly traded companies, blackout periods are used to prevent insider trading. Senior management, directors, and other employees may be prohibited from buying or selling company securities during the blackout because they have access to material, nonpublic information. A company may impose recurring blackout periods each quarter during the days before the earnings release. Non-recurring blackouts also may occur when the company encounters major changes that materially affect its immediate or long-term performance. Such events include mergers and acquisitions, an imminent release of a new product or service, or even an initial public offering by a private firm.

Transparency

Transparency may not remove asymmetry, but it provides shareholders assurance that all relevant information will be communicated to them. To avoid systemic bias, any information that would make a difference to the shareholder (with respect to their investment in the company) should be revealed concurrently to all interested parties, thus removing asymmetry instantaneously across all affected parties. Partially addressing information asymmetry, e.g., by sending a tweet, would mean some interested parties are left out from being informed, causing them to be at a probable disadvantage. Leaving out any of the shareholders or shareholder group violates the criterion of transparency, or openness in communication.

The board in its communication with shareholders must exhibit the highest level of transparency possible. While this is a laudable goal, challenges could surface in practicing the principle. For example, if the CEO or Chair of the board is terminally ill, the board should respect the confidentiality and privacy of the individual about whom the communication is concerned. An influential business leader who has built a thriving company may not have an apparent successor, at least in the eyes of the shareholder. So, this information is critical to the shareholders; however, the board must exercise caution in how much to reveal about the CEO's illness. The most recognized case illustrating the sensitivity of the communication content and timing is that of Steve Jobs, a great innovator and an impactful business leader, who was seriously ill in his final days at the helm of Apple Computers. Jobs made Apple into an enormous success story; for investors, Steve Jobs and Apple were synonymous. It was important for them to know about his health. And yet, doubts remain whether Apple board communicated to shareholders accurate and timely information about Jobs's health. The board may have had in mind a potential precipitous decline in Apple's share price if a dire picture about his health was painted for the shareholders. Importantly, the privacy of the person involved is to be respected; it may not be legally appropriate to disclose in detail the medical condition of a top executive. In sum, such situations are tough for the board to handle; what one would expect is the best exercise of their judgment while recognizing the need for transparency in their communication with shareholders. The opaqueness in communication in measured amounts may be well intentioned and appropriate.

Relevance and Clarity

Any information relayed to investors must be perceived as relevant to the shareholders. In fact, the concept of relevance of information is almost synonymous to the word information, that is, what is not relevant is not information to the recipient. If apparently relevant information is worded in a confusing manner involving technical jargon, for example, it may fail to serve the purpose for shareholders. As a result, a related requirement is that information should be as simply worded as possible without losing its meaning.

MEANS OF COMMUNICATION

There are several media or channels available to public companies to communicate with their shareholders. Perhaps the most recognized outlet is the SEC, where all public companies upload their filings in various formats (Word, PDF, EXCEL, XBRL). Some of these are on a cyclical basis; for example, quarterly financial statements (10Qs) are posted at the end of each quarter of the company's fiscal year, and the annual report (10K) is filed after the end of fiscal year. Since 10K is much broader in scope than just the annual report, most companies wrap the annual report information around their 10K as part of the annual communication with shareholders. Changes that bear economic consequences to the company are reported as they occur, rather than including them in the next report in the cycle. Similarly, events related to corporate governance (director appointment, resignation; insider trading reports) are reported as they happen (8K filing).

For shareholder communication, it is best to avoid certain media, such as the social media networks (e.g., Twitter, LinkedIn, Facebook). A widely held belief is that such media may not yet reach almost every shareholder, who may prefer to not belong to such a network for various reasons (e.g., cost, skills required, information security concerns). It is true, however, that the usage of technology will continue to become prominent in shareholder communication. Many companies have begun to promote paperless communication as in the electronic distribution of the proxy.

Management, specifically the CEO-CFO team, holds quarterly and year-end teleconferences to discuss financial performance and reasons for deviations from expected outcomes (for example, earnings guidance), and what the company is planning going forward. This is an opportunity for management to give "color" to the reported numbers for shareholders to comprehend the drivers behind the reported results, while at the same time answering shareholders' and analysts' questions. Although management would not normally reveal any strategic moves, it may discuss specific issues and challenges on hand and how the company is addressing them. General Electric, for example, has been going through significant changes, dropping segments like energy and revamping its financial services segment. While the press may have discussed some or all of these, it is management's responsibility to address these accurately, and in a timely manner, to the shareholders.

Earnings Guidance

A popular, although not mandatory, option companies have is to provide earnings guidance for the upcoming year, normally broken down into quarterly estimates of revenue and operating margins or some equivalent measures. Seasoned, stronger companies with a solid performance record may not opt to provide guidance; they may provide some projections and let the investors project likely bottom-line outcomes. However, most young, relatively small companies prefer to provide the guidance and, when circumstances change, revise the projections, giving explanations. For a company facing significant levels of uncertainty, providing earnings guidance could create challenges, for management will have to explain deviations from the guidance which are likely to arise. Regardless, earnings guidance offers an anchor to investors and molds their expectations regarding short-term financial performance.

The Proxy

The proxy statement is the principal avenue for the corporation to seek shareholder votes on various actions, both routine and non-routine. The proxy process is intended to mirror what would happen in an "in-person" meeting of shareholders, for the attendance at annual shareholders' meetings is low. There are very few exceptions, such as the Berkshire Hathaway annual general meeting with about 40,000 investors attending. It is therefore important for the proxy statement to communicate all information relevant for the shareholder to exercise the voting right. The needs of investors are a primary concern in designing the proxy. Conceptually, one could surmise that a shareholder absent at the annual meeting should not be penalized; to the extent possible, the shareholder's *in absentia* participation in the proceedings of the company should be guaranteed.

Driven by state laws, SEC regulations, other laws and regulations (e.g., Dodd-Frank Act), stock exchange listing requirements, and bylaws of the corporation, a proxy statement is a complex document that communicates with shareholders and seeks their vote of various resolutions. Table 12.2 lists typical, but not exhaustive, content included in a proxy document prepared for the annual general meeting. Other instances of proxy statements could arise, for example, when a major business transaction such as a merger is under consideration.

SHAREHOLDER ENGAGEMENT

Engaging shareholders is a laudable goal, but it presents a challenging task for the board and management. There are several reasons contributing to this challenge. Having delegated the task for governance on their behalf, shareholders may not have time, interest, or knowhow to intervene. They may perceive lack of influence of their ownership interest on the board or management, and may resort to the stock market to express their dissatisfaction with company performance. Despite such limitations, shareholder engagement is on the rise. While in some sense it might be considered a hindrance to the board or management, shareholder engagement could result in positive outcomes, or at least a better understanding of issues between shareholders and the board.

A first step to an effective shareholder engagement is for the board and management to understand the profile of shareholders. The shareholder profile would include views of the ownership from different angles. For example, such views would include shareholder type (institution, mutual fund, individual investor), insider versus outsider,

TABLE 12.2 Typical content of an annual proxy statement

A. An annual report

   1. Audited consolidated financial statements

   2. Selected financial information for the last five years.

   3. Management's discussion of financial condition at the end of the fiscal year and results of operations for the fiscal year

B. Executive officers and directors

   a. Named Executive Officers (NEOs): Names, ages, positions held with the company, business experience

   b. Directors: Names, ages, statement regarding independence, compensation, etc.

C. Audit Committee disclosures, including

   1. Related person transactions

   2. Charter

   3. Whether the member meets the requirement of the Audit Committee Financial Expert (ACFE)

D. Disclosures about each source of market risk

E. Business

   1. Nature and scope of the business

   2. Financial information about business segments

F. Shareholder returns

   1. Quarter-end common share prices and dividends declared in the last two fiscal years

(*Continued*)

TABLE 12.2 (Cont.)

G. Compensation and Disclosure Analysis (CD&A)

H. Shareholder votes

   1. Director election

   2. Say-on-Pay

   3. Ratification of the appointment of an independent auditor

I. Shareholder proposals

J. Other disclosures

   1. Whether the company has adopted a code of ethics, how it can be accessed, and if it covers principal executive officer, principal financial officer, and principal accounting officer or controller.

---

concentration (percentage of outstanding shares owned by top ten, top 20 shareholders, etc.), objective (if data are available, percent of owners aiming at aggressive growth, growth, value, income, etc.), location (by regions of the world), and by advisors and funds (top ten, for example). It is also important to review the dynamics of ownership over time, how it is changing, and what can be inferred from the change regarding future shareholder engagement.

If 90% of Corporation A's ownership is with individual investors and 90% of Corporation B's ownership belongs to institutional shareholders, shareholder engagement at A would likely be handled differently than at B. There may be few active individual investors at A, while institutional investors at B could be actively engaged with the board and management. After all, institutional investors are managing others' money in addition to their own, and would be responsible for fiduciary duty toward their client investees. Corporation A may find that it has many passive investors and only a small minority of them exercise a proxy vote. In 2013, retail investors voted only 30% of their public company shares, while institutional investors voted 90% of their shares.

Aside from addressing shareholder concerns, a more critical aspect of governance rests in proactively searching for and addressing any potential issues on the horizon. To identify shareholder influence, the board should periodically review the investor groups with significant investment in the voting stock of the company. Where the founder(s) and their affiliates hold a majority of voting stock, this may not make any difference to the board and management. However, in almost all cases, it would help determine the emerging influence of groups of investors, including hedge funds, who may become active in shaping future governance agenda, board membership, or executive leadership.

In the ordinary course, shareholders have the right to vote on several counts. This would provide feedback to the board for future action. If this routine process fails to have an impact of shareholder expectations, shareholder activism could come about.

Shareholder Votes

One normal pathway for shareholder engagement is shareholder votes, discussed in Chapter 7. While shareholder votes are not directly binding on the corporation, they do enhance accountability. Research shows that corporate boards pay close attention to the voting results and will seek to avoid "no" votes greater than 25–30%. Even if the board does not make any immediate change in response to shareholder repudiation, it would likely consider the outcome seriously in its future moves.

Shareholder Proposals

The choices in shareholder votes are normally put forth by the board and the shareholders are essentially voicing their opinion. Shareholder proposals flow in the other direction, where owners ask for a change by suggesting a particular action. Shareholder proposals are discussed in Chapter 7.

SHAREHOLDER ACTIVISM

In addition to the normal communication in compliance with regulatory requirements, shareholders often are in touch with the company primarily through its Investor Relations division. Whereas this is organized to address any shareholder's queries, it becomes even more critical in managing the concerns of those who garner significant ownership, usually around 5% of the company's outstanding voting stock, for such investors, including hedge funds, could disrupt the company.

A shareholder activist is a person who attempts to use his or her rights as a shareholder of a public company to bring about change within or for the company. Over the past decades and especially since the 1970s, several activists made shareholder activism a viable and impactful means of change in the corporate world. Carl Icahn, Bill Ackman, David Einhorn, and Dan Loeb are among the activists well recognized among investors. Most of these activists are turnaround investors, entering the scene and effecting change relatively quickly, and then perhaps exiting – all in a matter of five years or less. When an activist begins to own voting shares in a company, the signs are very clear that a change is about to happen. The probability that changes made would help improve shareholder returns is perceived to be high. As a result, the entry of an activist on the roster of a company shareholder is considered a positive signal. "Icahn lift," for example, is the stock price effect that occurs when Carl Icahn begins to purchase shares in a company.

Early activism was the disdain of the board and management. An activist's presence at the company door was considered "bad news," because the investor would raise issues, make the board and management accept adjustments to their conduct, tactics, or strategy, promote efficiency, and ask for a voice on the board. Any such concerns would be heard by the board since the activist owns a recognizable share of outstanding shares of the company. Significant ownership is a source of shareholder activism, whether friendly or hostile in its overtures to management and the board. Figure 12.1 presents a conceptual view of shareholder activism.

Shareholder activism has been growing over time. According to a report by World Economic Forum, the number of activist activities grew from 520 in 2013 to 758 in 2016. The report informs that in 1976, shareholders held shares for 5.1 years on average in the USA (3.9 years globally); comparable 2015 figures are 7.4 (7.3) months. This may cause investors to set goals of significant returns within a short period of time; as a result, focus on how shareholders could gain outsize returns in the immediate term makes them myopic in their attitude. If such goals are

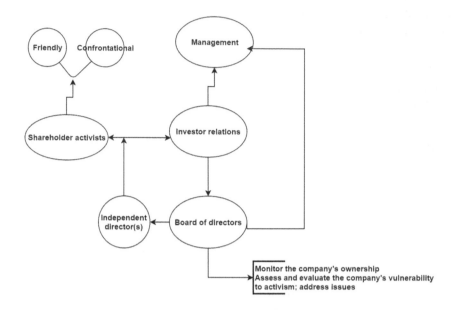

FIGURE 12.1   Shareholder activism.

not realized, shareholders may tend to disagree with management on how it runs the company and suggest steps that may result in considerable disruption in the path that the company follows. Active shareholders often suggest the firing of current board member(s) and may opt to have their choice elected to the board.

What started as a short-term activism has been changing, moving more in the direction of achieving long-term shareholder returns. As a result, many of the moves suggested by constructive activists are focused on improving the company, perhaps even shrinking its scope of operations, selling assets, improving the board dynamics, and causing greater innovation and change at the top levels. And there are more of them, including more institutional investors, joining the activism revolution.

Regardless of time orientation, there is a positive side to shareholder activism. When expectations are not met, there exist underlying reasons, perceived or real, that the activists believe are causing the expectation gap. Slowing sales, shrunken margins, acquisitions at outsized price tags are among the many that the activists might believe, based on their analysis and reflection, contribute to the expectation gap. If real, management benefits from such perspectives by addressing them or, if already acted upon, by communicating steps management is taking; if imagined, management can communicate reality and comfort the activists that things are in order. At a minimum, management and the board, initially working through Investor Relations, must listen to their concerns. Not paying attention or showing total disregard, even where it is legal, would only worsen the situation and may cause distraction to management. In extreme cases, the board, through its independent directors normally perceived to be objective, works on resolving the shareholder concerns.

Those in charge of governance, especially the board, must be proactive in their actions. If the board acts in a timely manner and communicates effectively with the shareholders, there may not be room for the activists to rise. The board must assess and evaluate the company's vulnerability to activism and deliberately exercise oversight on the vulnerable points. For each company, the triggers generating vulnerability could be different. Generally, all such triggers have to do with out-of-the-norm visibility of the company compared to its peers. Examples include underperforming lines of business or the materiality of nonoperating assets that could otherwise be monetized, disproportionately large intangible assets or intellectual property, stock's trading range relative to that of peers, management compensation (perceived to be out of the norm), or a long tenure of the board that is perceived to be weak. A periodic assessment along these lines would alert the board of signs of future conflict with influential shareholders. More importantly, such an exercise would help identify specific steps to take where the issue is real and is impacting the company's performance.

Shareholder Derivative Suit

As owner, a shareholder can represent the company in a lawsuit since the rights of the shareholder are derived from the rights of the company itself. In cases where a shareholder believes that harm is done to the company, perhaps by those who have been trusted to run the company (board, management), the shareholder may, on behalf of the company, sue the defendant for damages. A derivative legal action may arise from any alleged wrongdoing by the board, management, or both. An example is the rejection of an attractive buyout offer by the board, presumably causing shareholders to sacrifice potential gains from the sale of the company. The plaintiff in a derivative action represents the company (that is, all shareholders) and damages recovered go to the company, not the shareholder suing on behalf of the company. Finally, in some states, the shareholder considering a derivative action must make a pre-suit demand to the party causing the alleged harm to redress the situation, unless such an attempt is likely to prove fruitless.

Class Action Suit

A class action suit is by shareholders of a particular class (e.g., those who held shares in the company between certain dates, signifying the critical event or its impact); a class action is for and on behalf of the entire class, unless any shareholders choose to opt out of it. The purpose is to allow numerous shareholders to claim for damages even under conditions where individual damages are insignificant. Class action suits tend to eliminate redundancy in litigation and thus improve efficiency. Each case must have a common legal issue and those who bring action must represent the entire class of shares, except in cases where investors voluntarily opt out of the action.

The field of shareholder engagement is vast, impacted over time by market forces, the law and regulations, shareholder influence, and the board and management conduct. In future, the topic is likely to gain more traction. A wide array of options could surface from investors in order to protect their investment and ensure that it generates satisfactory returns. It appears that the shareholder activism in the public company environment is becoming more like the functioning of a private equity company, with little interest in anything but cutting waste, streamlining operations, removing incompetent managers, and driving results. Private company owners can move fast and have direct impact on the company; the public company has to endure a longer due process because management is clearly separated from the investors.

BIBLIOGRAPHY

Breitinger, D. What is shareholder activism and how should businesses respond? World Economic Forum. www.weforum.org/agenda/2017/08/shareholder-activism-business-response-explainer, Accessed June 7, 2019.

Ernst & Young. 2019. *2019 Proxy Statements: An Overview of the Requirements and Observations about Current Practice.* Ernst & Young. www.ey.com/publication/vwluassetsdld/2019proxystatements_05133-181us_6december2018-v2/$file/2019proxystatements_05133-181us_6december2018-v2.pdf?OpenElement, Accessed October 23, 2019.

Gillan, S. L. and Starks, L. T. 2007. The evolution of shareholder activism in the United States. *The Journal of Applied Corporate Finance* 19(1): 55–73.

Ruggeri, C. Shareholder activism and the role of the board. *The CFO Journal,* April 30, 2019. https://deloitte.wsj.com/cfo/2019/04/30/shareholder-activism-and-the-role-of-the-board/, Accessed June 7, 2019.

Securities and Exchange Commission, Release No. 34–81916; File No. PCAOB-2017-01, October 23, 2017.

CHAPTER 13

Organizational Wrongdoing

Organizational wrongdoing includes an improper or unethical act on the part of any member or members of the organization. A long-held belief is that such wrongdoing is an anomaly; it indeed appears so. However, a more recent outlook on it suggests that such wrongdoing is a normal phenomenon, and happens all the time in the conduct of an organization. Examples include the Volkswagen's manipulation of monitoring auto emissions, Toshiba's manipulation of results in line with budgets, and Wells Fargo's autocratic push for issuing payment cards to existing customers without their asking for it. Add to this list Boeing's 737 MAX story, where it appears that due diligence exercised by regulators overly trusted the regulated entity!

This chapter covers how compromises in organizations occur. The framework used to explain the phenomenon is the disposition-based fraud model (DFM), a recently developed model that lays out components and their relationships in an act of any kind of indulgence. The discussion includes possible reasons for such wrongdoings and how the corporate governance roles, specifically the external auditor and the board, can prevent or detect such white collar crimes.

DISPOSITION-BASED FRAUD MODEL (DFM)

White collar crime has been around for a long time. Included among such crimes is financial fraud in the form of actual misappropriation of the organization's assets or misreporting or manipulation of financial numbers. Most attempts to describe financial fraud use an early empirical model called the fraud triangle. In its basic form, the fraud triangle suggests that a culmination of three conditions potentially signal a financial fraud: opportunity, incentives and pressure, and attitudes or rationalization. Although adopted widely in the auditing pronouncements (e.g., see AICPA's AU-C Section 240), the explanatory power of the fraud triangle is limited. As a result, we discuss in detail an alternative model, called the disposition-based fraud model (DFM). The DFM, while generally applicable, concerns powerful influencers in the corporate governance arena, especially the chief executive and the chief financial officer.

The DFM is based on the premise that every human act involves interaction between the human being and the circumstances; an act of fraud belongs to this same nucleus. It is therefore logical to project a fraudulent act as a similar interaction with the final outcome being financial fraud. The scenario involves two roughly independent parts: the human choice to indulge (the actor side) and the circumstances surrounding the act (the action side).

The Actor

Temptations are everywhere; people indulge in temptations and thus make choices, including moral and nonmoral choices. The DFM proposes that humans fight inclinations contrary to moral choices, but could break down and indulge in moral temptations. Table 13.1 illustrates the situation using a simple scenario.

A high degree of vulnerability to moral temptation arises from a self-regarding (SR) disposition of the person. In contrast, people of other-regarding (OR) disposition are relatively safe from such moral temptations and can successfully fight the urge to compromise. Thus, the model posits that the SR disposition has a greater risk of falling prey to moral temptations. However, this presumed relationship is subject to moderating effects of self-control. The greater the self-control, the more likely that vulnerability to temptation can be overcome. However, where self-control is temporarily negatively impacted by ego depletion (a demanding effort of self-control leaving one with less to effectively cope with the next challenge), the executive, particularly of SR disposition, would

TABLE 13.1 Temptations and compromises

My daughter's pet, a chihuahua, is a loving, cute little dog. Because she came home in October, she was named Pumpkin. I used to take her out for a walk in the evening. Somedays, I wouldn't feel like going with her, but then she needed the walk and I was the only one around!

During the walk, Pumpkin would normally go potty. I would pick up the stool in a plastic bag and put it in a garbage can; of course, it is the right thing to do. Acting otherwise would be considered improper behavior. However, some evenings when I didn't feel quite up to it, I would leave the potty in place and walk away. I may have had my own rationalizations when I did that; for example, "I am tired," "My back hurts," or "It is too dark to notice the semi-liquid defecation." The fact was that I compromised my moral duty and indulged in an inappropriate behavior.

Regardless of the excuses, the behavior as such is triggered by my disposition, categorized as either self-regarding or other-regarding. The former types are more vulnerable to abandon their morals.

Self-control often is a counteracting force that may prevent a person from doing the wrong thing. However, self-control tends to deplete when exercised throughout the day. Also, the closer I get to the temptation, the less likely that I will pay attention to anything but the temptation. The urge to indulge overwhelms me.

To prevent such socially undesirable behavior, my neighborhood association might hire services of "poop patrol," a watchdog that stores genetic maps of the refuse of all pets in the neighborhood, and when an excrement is found, determines which pet's owner violated the norm. In essence, regulators and planned obstacles step in where compromises are likely. Then the cat-and-mouse act begins: the actor tries to hide the indulgence while the neighbor association attempts to unearth the wrongdoing. Cover up requires an exercise of self-efficacy, one's capacity to conceal.

In terms of characteristics, temptations and compromises are no different in the corporate arena. The model applies to the financial fraud as much as it does to a minor indulgence of not picking up the "poop."

likely be tempted to indulge in an unethical act. Self-control may be rendered ineffective when psychological inertia sets in. As the actor approaches a temptation, the closer he gets, the greater the grip of temptation, making him incapable of withstanding the attraction.

A person's disposition, which determine proneness and tendencies, affects one's choices and is shaped by the person's moral identity, which can be categorized as either symbolic moral identity or internal moral identity. The former is reflected in adherence to laws and regulations, and the latter, in inner conscious convictions. Arguably, SR appears to align with symbolic moral identity and OR, internal moral identity. Each is significantly related to self-control. However, individuals with more internal moral identities show higher levels of self-control strength than the individuals with more symbolic moral identities. In the DFM, this would substantiate the supposition that OR disposition is likely supported by more self-control strength than the SR disposition. Finally, among leaders who have low moral identity (presumably SRs), depletion of self-control could contribute to unethical behaviors.

A moral compromise occurs due to a judgment shift, that is, the agent perceives that immediate payoffs of indulgence now are greater than the long-term rewards of resisting the temptation. This is an evaluation that may be influenced by the person's affective state at the time. Often called managerial myopia, the driver of judgment shift is essentially the manager's tendency to overrate the immediate at the cost of the long-term good.

The Action

In part, the actor's assessment of obstacles to the indulgence (e.g., internal controls) in light of the actor's possible maneuvers that could effectively neutralize the obstacles (self-efficacy in the DFM) could stifle the process of judgment shift. For example, if the agent cannot conceive of self-efficacy measures to overcome relevant obstacles to the indulgence, he might refrain from acting immorally. Self-efficacy implies that the manager has capability to commit the fraud and subsequently conceal it as well. In the absence of the fraudster's efficacy, it is unlikely that many frauds would have occurred. Self-efficacy measures suggest specific capabilities the fraudster chooses to activate in a fraud situation. Unlike obstacles, most of which the company plans and implements in the form of ICFR, self-efficacy measures are chosen by the perpetrator in each case.

Finally, upon indulgence, *ex post* rationalizations supporting the immoral choice are likely. Rationalization can be considered as the mental exercise of justifying one's nonmoral conduct or decision with a view to reducing the negative emotions that accompany such decisions. A conceptual view of the DFM appears in Figure 13.1. To demonstrate the value of DFM in financial fraud analysis, the case of Satyam Computers is included in Table 13.2.

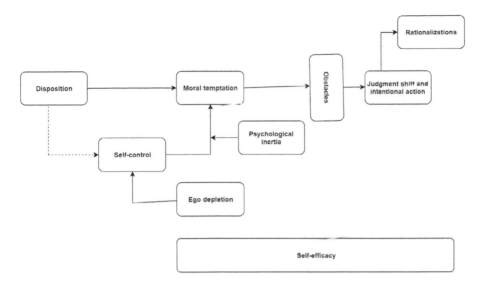

FIGURE 13.1 Disposition-based fraud model (DFM).

Source: V. Raval. 2018. A disposition-based fraud model: Theoretical integration and research agenda, *Journal of Business Ethics* 150(3): 741–763. Adapted with permission from Springer publications.

TABLE 13.2 Satyam Computer Services

Founded in 1987, Satyam Computer Services Private Limited (Satyam) was in the business of outsourcing information technology skills and services. In 1991, the company was converted into a public limited company. Following deregulation of such services accompanied by tax incentives from the Government of India in early 1990s, Satyam experienced a huge growth spurt in the following years. The Raju family that founded the business in Hyderabad, India, controlled the destiny of the company. Mr. Ramalinga Raju, the founder of Satyam and chairman of its board, quickly gained reputation for excellent leadership with integrity in charting Satyam's future.

The Satyam board in 2008 was comprised of five "independent" directors and four non-independent directors (Raju and his brother, an employee, and a consultant for Satyam). It is doubtful if all independent directors were truly independent. The audit committee of Satyam, comprised of four independent directors, met eight times in 2008. The committee's conduct appeared to suggest total compliance with rules and regulations, that is, the "I's were dotted, and T's were crossed appropriately."

(Continued)

TABLE 13.2 (Cont.)

With impressive financial growth since inception, expectations of continued growth among investors were high. However, worldwide recessionary trends in 2008 slowed the economy, adding to Raju's concerns about maintaining consistent growth at Satyam. Perhaps the sluggish growth surfaced sooner than the year 2008; according to Raju, the manipulation of financial results continued over a much longer period of time. The SEC in its complaint (2011) alleged of the impropriety from at least 2003 through September 2008. The high-level misreporting became possible with Raju recruiting the company CFO for the act. The primary means used to cook the books was the use of super-user privilege to record fictitious transactions in the accounting system.

For all practical purposes, a large majority of those in charge of governance were not independent. Raju certainly was conflicted, with involvement of his family in the company management and with several significant related party transactions. The company approved outsize audit fees for the auditors, rendering them conflicted and myopic with their lax audit practices.

With his largely self-regarding charity, Raju projected himself as a strong steward of his stakeholders, especially in the local community. No one would believe or could challenge his good motives. With a high level of trust endowed due to his reputation, it was possible for Raju to get his way with practically anyone whom he wanted to recruit for a wrongdoing.

The "straw that broke the camel's back" was the proposal to merge Mytas properties and Mytas infrastructure, where Raju and his family members are a related party, with Satyam. Such a merger appeared to have the potential to wash out any created gap in the numbers at Satyam with hard real estate assets from Mytas that the proposed merger would bring. Shareholders did not agree with the proposal. The options left for Raju was to either continue with the numbers game until it was exposed or admit the wrongdoing.

Upon release of his letter to the Satyam board, the share price tumbled 78%. On January 9, 2009, Raju was arrested. Soon after, his brother (B. Rama Raju) and the Satyam CFO (S. Vadlamani) were arrested. The Government of India replaced the entire board and proceeded to find a "home" for the salvageable portions of Satyam.

REASONS FOR FINANCIAL FRAUD

As long as temptations exist, financial frauds are likely to surface for various reasons. Organizational wrongdoing is a norm rather than just one-off deviant behavior. Also, self-regarding disposition of executives is likely to make them more vulnerable to moral temptations. There is some degree of overlap between such dispositions and narcissistic personality traits, especially those involving the notion of entitlement. A majority of successful executives are likely to exhibit high levels of narcissism, leading to a greater chance of financial fraud. If an executive deliberating a fraud can find ways to counter potentially relevant internal controls, or any other obstacles to such an act, there is a chance that the fraud would occur.

Many researchers advocate that pressures on executives cause them to indulge in a compromise. The problem is, pressure is internal to the person. How well the individual will be able to withstand such pressure to not indulge in inclinations contrary to his moral duty seems to be a matter of personal disposition and self-control. For example, self-regarding executives are likely to be more vulnerable to immoral acts while other-regarding executives are better positioned to withstand such temptations. While it is easy to blame pressure, high-level executives should be responsible to manage internal pressures in the public interest; it is their duty to do so.

Measures to Detect or Prevent Fraud

Most fraud deterrents, if at all effective, can only detect financial fraud; there are few, if any, measures available to prevent such fraud. The most viable systemwide detective control that the Sarbanes-Oxley Act requires of every public company is a whistleblower system. An anonymous tip left in the system can be accessed by appropriate authority, such as the chair of the audit committee of the board, that is also responsible to follow up and address the concern noted in the tip. The entire sequence from the receipt of the tip through the final action taken must be documented. Such documentation, when analyzed for the root causes of control system failure, can be used to further improve internal controls of the company.

The DFM reveals that executive compensation structure is an important preventive measure. This is because if the structure is biased toward rewarding the executive for the short-term performance, it would facilitate the judgment shift. Looking at the work of the compensation committee of the board, one could determine how the executive long-term compensation is pegged against her short-term (immediate) compensation. If the ratio of long-term rewards to immediate reward is low, it would enhance the executive's perception that current rewards are more attractive than future rewards; this may lead to judgment shift, a move encouraging managerial myopia and thus leading to the fraud. Such innovative perspective on long- versus short-term executive compensation is currently missing or is rare; it appears the compensation committee works in isolation of the audit committee. The risk of managerial myopia presumably causing judgment shift is not yet on the list of the audit committee or the external auditor.

One rich source of understanding corporate executive fraud is the human side of such acts. Although somewhat difficult for the business professional to appreciate its practical usefulness, an additional promising area of preventive measures comes from understanding the executive's disposition. A self-regarding disposition is vulnerable to promoting organizational wrongdoing. In respect of senior managers, Warren Buffett in his 2002 letter to shareholders contends that "when management takes the low road in aspects that are visible, it is likely they are following a similar path behind the scenes." Simply, the self-regarding tendencies cannot apply in just one place but not the other. Thus, it would help to study the executive in both formal and social contexts to understand his tendencies and proneness. While such executives may be highly successful in their business performance, they may also be highly vulnerable to commit a compromise. Presumably, one could help them guard against their weakness and thereby assist in avoiding corporate meltdown.

If a company is in the market for a replacement of the chief executive, the purpose is to recruit the best candidate for the job. The board, with the help of human resource management function, should conduct a succession exercise, and in the process, review possible candidates within for all key positions in the company. Knowing the disposition of an internal candidate for promotion is probably much easier than that of an outside candidate. And yet, one should recognize that in recruiting a CEO, there are many factors to consider, not just the disposition of the candidate, and the board may choose to look outside the company. However, the board must recognize the risk of selecting someone who is vulnerable to cutting corners on ethical behavior.

ROLE OF AUDITORS

It is recognized that external auditors are not directly responsible for finding fraud. However, if a fraud has been committed or is in progress, auditors are required to exercise due diligence. If evidence examined in the course of an audit leads to the possibility that a financial fraud might have occurred, the auditors should investigate further. Regulatory agencies typically would presume that auditors in their role are best positioned, both from their role as well as professional competencies, to unearth any wrongdoing. In recent years, the responsibility to detect fraudulent activity has been extended to areas normally considered outside the purview of a financial audit. For example, the SEC asked the auditors of Wells Fargo to explain why they failed to detect the auditee's aggressive stance toward opening new accounts, or issuing credit cards, not authorized by their existing customers.

To meet these expectations, auditors have added new, or expanded existing, audit techniques. Clearly, the trend is to move away from a checklist approach and institute or improve brainstorming techniques to unearth any corporate compromises. Typically, the roles that come under the auditor's microscope are those of the CEO and CFO, although other leadership roles may also come under scrutiny.

While the current wave of new approaches is data driven, auditors are likely to benefit equally from focusing on the human side of crimes. The DFM model suggests that although qualitative, an examination and evaluation of the executive's disposition could lead to potential red flags. This is not necessarily a one-time exercise, but rather an ongoing effort to understand the moral identity of those involved in steering the corporation from the top.

Psychopath and narcissist roles within the organizational contexts have been examined. A broad understanding is that executives exhibiting such tendencies could be highly successful in their roles, but at the same time they are also prone to committing compromises. In assessing a leader's disposition, it is not necessary to ask the leader about his or her disposition; the behavioral trail itself could produce strong evidence of the executive's disposition. Now there are surrogate measures of narcissism available to determine a person's disposition; for example, if the executive's philanthropic profile is geared toward promoting the self, chances are, he is of self-regarding disposition. Additionally, auditors have access to related party transactions of the company. Instead of just focusing on the amount and its materiality, auditors could decipher the intentions behind such transactions by visualizing the structure, implicit purpose, and the beneficiary of such transactions. For example, Adelphia's related party transactions were meant to benefit the inner circle of executives, while Berkshire does not entertain any such transactions unless they clearly benefit the company. We Company, the parent of WeWork, was planning in 2019 to go public. Initial valuation of the company was marked at $45 billion. However, the founder chairman and CEO's self-regarding behavior became apparent in the SEC filing for the IPO. Included among the leader's incursions were related party transactions, purchase of company shares with a loan from the company, nepotism, and sale of rights to the company name owned by the leader. Investor apathy toward the company grew. The IPO was deferred, valuation sank to about $8 billion, and the leader was pushed out of his central role at We Company.

ROLE OF THE BOARD

The board of directors as a body representing shareholders' interests is responsible to protect the assets of the company and to actively mitigate the risk of a financial fraud. The stakes are high because any incidence of fraud would cause the company reputational loss, loss of market value and consequent degradation in seeking financial resources (a bank loan, for example), loss of focus from executing corporate strategy, and so on. Once a fraud occurs, the time and resources it takes to wipe out its impact could be enormous.

Although members of the board are not always around management, they still have a better and perhaps longer window of exposure to the executive leadership compared to the external auditors. Board members have a better chance of comprehending the disposition of top leaders via behavioral leads picked up from formal and social encounters with the executives. Besides, the board evaluates top leadership frequently and should also conduct succession planning exercises regularly. They know reasonably well the performance potential and moral fabric of each manager likely to be considered for promotion to higher levels of accountability. As a result, they should be able to keep the company's leadership on high moral grounds through their recommendations for internal development of leadership potential.

Because financial fraud often happens at the top level, it is necessary for the board to watch high-level systemwide obstacles or controls that could detect or prevent such indiscretions. Whistleblower provisions are an important obstacle that rises above all, including the top executives. Therefore, effective implementation of the system is very important to expose any incidents. There is, of course, a risk of receiving an erroneous report, but overall, the benefits are much greater than the cost. To encourage reporting, employees should be assured of anonymity and promised there will be no backlash on account of filing the incident. Obstacles of this nature and beyond reach of the executives should be identified and implemented to minimize exposure to corporate wrongdoing of any kind.

Once an act of fraud is detected or even suspected, the board should take immediate steps to learn more about the compromise, how it occurred, and who seems to be the primary party to the wrongdoing. During this time, appropriate communication with the shareholders and regulators is necessary, and the employees should also be informed of the development. Crises happen. Organizational wrongdoing is more of a norm than an exception, and the efforts should be toward managing the risk as best as the board can do.

FUTURE DIRECTIONS IN FORENSICS

Those in charge of governance, including accounting and auditing professionals, are likely to find that they need out-of-the-box approaches to detect financial fraud. This is because the act of fraud is a complex event that involves many factors, both quantitative and qualitative. The traditional checklist approach is unlikely to work. Both financial and non-financial data, as also hard and soft data, should be analyzed and, where appropriate, data analytics should be used to gain insights.

Regulators will have to look beyond internal controls. Since the override of internal controls is possible by senior executives, it is necessary to enrich regulations in innovative ways. An example is the whistleblower system. However, simply putting more and more emphasis on controls is going to become less and less cost effective. Although the law might pay less attention to the human side of crime and more to the punishment of violators, the room for improvement lies equally on the side of the actor that commits the wrong. There is more to gain from understanding human behavior and applying it to future means of governance.

An argument that professional accountants and auditors are not behavioral economists is going to fall short. Professionals will have to learn about the nature and importance of innovative forensics to prevent or detect fraud, and this will include the human psyche. The emphasis on the human side of fraud could certainly prove quite helpful in developing a complete metrics to unearth corporate wrongdoings.

BIBLIOGRAPHY

Holton, R. 2009. *Willing, Wanting, Waiting* (eBook). Oxford, England: Oxford University Press.

Joosten, A., van Dijke, M., van Hiel, A. and De Cremer, D. 2014. Being "in control" may make you lose control: the role of self-regulation in unethical leadership behavior. *Journal of Business Ethics* 121: 1–14.

Palmer, D. A. 2013.The new perspective on organizational wrongdoing. *California Management Review* 56(1): 5–23.

Raval, V. 2018. A disposition-based fraud model: Theoretical integration and research agenda. *Journal of Business Ethics* 150(3): 741–763.

Raval, V. and Raval, V. 2019a. Self-regarding disposition as a fraud-risk factor and its relationship with narcissism, a working paper.

Raval, V. and Raval, V. 2019b. The *Truth* About Satyam. A working paper.

Rua, T., Lawter, L. and Andreassi, J. 2017. Desire to be ethical or ability to self-control: Which is more crucial to ethical behavior? *Business Ethics: A European Review* 26: 288–299.

IV

Other Topics

CHAPTER 14

Governance of Non-Public Organizations

In order to survive and thrive, organizations engage in risk management. In doing so, some are very structured and analytical in their approach, while others may be unstructured and heuristic. The smaller, unincorporated entities may be less consciously practicing risk management while the large businesses, especially public companies, usually adopt a systematic path to risk mitigation, partly because of the laws and regulations they are subject to. As we have seen, public companies resort to systemic governance to protect the interests of their shareholders. Regardless, the practice of governance is a sound way for any organization to manage risk; it leads to more predictable outcomes, with decreasing volatility from controllable factors. In sum, the idea of risk management, regardless of the beneficiary, is the same whether applied to public companies or any other organization.

While the focus of preceding chapters was on public companies, we now turn to non-public organizations. Non-public organizations include practically the universe of organizations with one exception: public companies. They represent a vast array of firms from convenience stores to very large global companies. Most businesses begin with a modest amount of capital, mainly from the owner and his or her family and friends. Perhaps the business is launched in the basement or garage of the owner's home. Non-public entities can be classified into three groups: family-owned businesses, private companies (excluding family businesses), and non-profit organizations. Much like a public company, the profit motive guides the first two; the third category stands out as one where directly profiting from operations is not the mission. Figure 14.1 illustrates the types of organizations and their risk management through governance.

For non-public entities, how the company is run or how it finances the business may not be subject to elaborate regulatory requirements. But even non-public companies have to manage the risk of owning and running the business. As a risk management strategy, if properly structured and managed, corporate governance practices will likely lead to long-term benefits regardless of the size or type of organization.

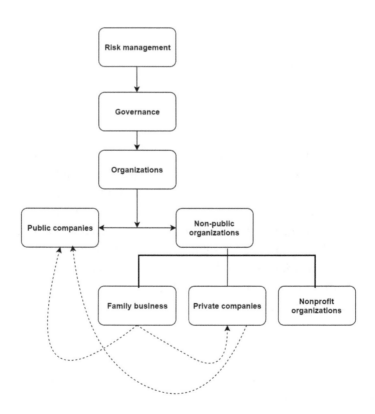

FIGURE 14.1   Public and non-public organizations.

When a small business grows into a much larger and more complex organization, the discipline imposed by adopted governance practices would facilitate transition to a large private company, and if desired, ultimately to a public company.

STAKEHOLDERS

A key difference across public and non-public companies is in terms of stakeholders. The principal stakeholder in a public company is the shareholder. For non-public companies, there is some variation in how one would view the primary stakeholder. A small family business has an owner and may even have some or all of the family members with ownership interests. A private company is more like a public company, with perhaps many investors as stakeholders. Investors in a private company often include company employees who own shares in the company. Private companies are closely held; they do not have the right to seek investment from investors at large. The shares of private companies are not listed on a stock exchange and cannot be publicly traded.

The final category, non-profit organizations, comprises mostly incorporated legal entities that pursue charitable causes and seek tax exempt status from the Internal Revenue Service. These include churches, temples, and synagogues, homeless shelters, art museums, private universities, and hospitals. Some of the most visible non-profits are Goodwill Industries International, United Way Worldwide, and the American Red Cross. The stakeholders of non-profits are generally the patrons or beneficiaries of the charity. Since non-profits depend on donations, another group of stakeholders is the donors.

STATUTORY GOVERNANCE REQUIREMENTS

Compared to public companies, it is true that fewer regulations apply to non-public companies. However, they are not entirely exempt from laws and regulations. Non-public companies are relatively "free" from fiduciary obligations in handling their operations and financing their assets. This is because they do not approach the financial markets in the same way as a public company does. This in turn results in fewer regulations for the non-public companies.

Because public companies lean on financial markets for generating capital, they have a fiduciary responsibility to the owners, that is, shareholders. Public company accountability is central to their shareholders' trust in the company and its management; to keep this trust, laws and regulations are necessary and enforcement of their compliance is warranted. No such formal agency relationship prevails in non-public organizations, for the owners are managers of the business risk. Where the separation of ownership from management is unclear, investors in all likelihood "call the shots," even when not involved in day-to-day management.

The applicable statutory requirements for non-public companies depend largely on how they are organized. If the owner has everything at risk and no outsider is involved in risk sharing through debt or ownership interests, there is less likelihood that statutory governance requirements would exist. On the other hand, looking for limited liability protection in its formation would imply that some degree of oversight might be imposed, for outside parties may be at risk.

One source of regulations is the state in which the entity is incorporated. Additionally, federal government regulations contribute to statutory requirements; among the many agencies, the one that imposes significant filing requirements is the IRS.

Regardless of how organized, it is important to look at the formation, structure and control, and governance challenges of each type of non-public organization. Where possible, this discussion includes comparisons with public companies.

FAMILY BUSINESS

A family-owned business (simply, family business) is an entity whose owners belong to a single family. As the family grows and children have their own family, the ownership interests may still remain within the extended family. There are three distinct forces at work in a family business: the family, the owners, and the business. Although the ownership may be vested within the family, not every family member may have been designated as owner, and the stakes of those who are owners may vary. As a result, it is necessary to consider the family and owners as separate forces affecting the entire family as a beneficiary of the business. The agency relationship can thus be implied between the family as the fiduciary beneficiary and the members of the family who are owners. The business is a separate entity; however, the distinction between business and home – especially in small businesses – may be fuzzy in making choices. Emotions and related party considerations may rule decisions to hire, issue contracts, and purchase resources or services. Business decisions affect the family and some of the family divisiveness may be borne out of who runs the business and how it is managed.

Some family businesses thrive, become very large, and stay as a private company or go public. Reliance Group in India, for example, has become a major conglomerate in India, despite the family split and discord among two brothers after the founder, Dhirubhai Ambani, died. Satyam Computers, until its demise due to financial fraud, was a shining example of how family businesses grow and contribute significantly to the nation's economy. Racine, Wisconsin-based S. C. Johnson company, founded in 1886, is still a family-led private company, a global manufacturer of household and professional products for cleaning, storage, air care, pest control, and shoe care.

Formation

Family businesses start small and have a simple ownership structure, such as sole proprietorship or partnership. Resources available to the business are limited and access to lenders is also limited. The risks are high and the chances of survival are minimal. The vision of the founder, persistence, and the ability to survive could ultimately lead to a viable business.

Since family business does not require a separate legal identity, the formation of the business may not involve much legal procedure or subsequent regulatory reporting. Business income may be reported as part of the personal income on the tax return. So, the legal requirements in the formation of family business may be minimal and relatively simple.

Structure and Control

Like any business, a family business needs discipline and monitoring. It sorely needs independent advice from those well-wishers of the family who have little vested interest in the business. At the very least, a sounding board could save the family and the business from the risks of ownership of the business.

A family business is invariably bonded with the owner-family. It is often hard to distinguish between the private life and work life of the owner. The owner has also the challenging task of balancing the interests of the rest of the family while protecting and preserving the business. The intertwined interests of business and personal life could cause a rift in the family. Objectivity and principled decision making may become a challenge. After all, the CEO, the accountant, and the operating manager may all belong to the same family, where open dialog and constructive feedback could be rare.

Family business governance runs the spectrum from informal, unstructured governance to a highly visible, structured, and formal governance. Right structure, appropriate processes, and right kind of people – candid, insightful in the world of business, and relatively independent of the family – could help the business. A board similar to one for the business, organized at the family level, is often called the family council. While optional, its presence could provide important feedback to the business board of advisors and, as well, to the family members.

Governance Challenges

Where most governance is discretionary, it is likely that least will be done, perhaps not because the owner is too busy or has low integrity, but rather due to the fact that it is perceived as not necessary at the time or that it is expensive. Compromises such as financial fraud or egregious spending are more likely in a family business. In one study, it was found that auditors assess the risk of fraud as higher for family firms than for non-family firms. Moreover, the study found that firms with weak audit committees have the highest fraud risk.

The most significant governance challenge in a family business comes from the need to balance the interests of the family, owners within the family, and the business. The three coexist and are dependent on each other. Relationships within the family may confound the issues; discussion may often be clouded by charged emotions that displace reason. Not being able to disagree with others or raise a fair voice on an important matter could signify "faultlines" among family members, may suffocate business growth, and drive a wedge within the family. Where open dialog and constructive conflict resolution become impossible, the business suffers.

As the founder's children grow and seek more voice in the operations, the generation gap could result in differences of opinion. Such differences can have a lasting impact on the business, for example, in the choice of business strategy or the debt leverage sought. Risk appetites across generations could vary and may surface deeper concerns regarding risk identification and management.

The founder ultimately would exit or become less active in the day-to -day affairs of the business. Choosing a successor at this point poses a major challenge. Who do you trust to lead the business? How do you select a family member for this role? Or do you go outside and recruit a non-family member for the position? The need to look outside for a successor could arise from the lack of interest in the business on the part of family members. On the flip side, there could be occasions where more than one family member shows an interest in leading the business, and picking one can be an emotional challenge.

Myriad other challenges could also surface. Someone wants to buy your business, alternative products or services are introduced by competitors, disruptive technology makes the business redundant and much less viable – these are all possible situations that could confront the founder.

Finally, having a good governance structure and a prestigious board may not necessarily mean business success. Theranos, a blood-testing company that touted breakthrough technology, became a widely known name and a rising star. Its leader, Elizabeth Holmes, was highly regarded as a leader in the healthcare industry. She was charismatic, confident, and convincing to a degree where stakeholders began trusting her word as truth. This is a graphic example of the executive's self-efficacy in neutralizing obstacles in the path of a wrongdoing. Besides, she appointed her boyfriend in charge of operations, thus removing possibilities that acts of indiscretion would be exposed. However, false claims concerning medical devices and suspect validity of laboratory test results caused a precipitous decline of Theranos. The valuation of the company, which was marked around $10 billion in 2013–2014, languished thereafter. The casualty rate in family-driven startups is very high, even when it is backed by funding from venture capitalists and private investors.

PRIVATE COMPANY

A private company is a firm subject to private ownership. In this sense, family businesses are private businesses, although discussed separately in this chapter. A family business can be incorporated as a private corporation at any time without giving up benefits for family ownership and control. Koch Industries has remained in the Koch family since its founding in 1940. A key benefit is that the company does not have to answer to its public shareholders. Alternatively, some family-owned companies have gone public and yet maintained control through a dual-class share structure, where the family owns the class with multiple votes per share owned.

Private companies have the choice of issuing stock and having share-holders, but their shares are not traded on stock exchanges. The issue of shares of stock to investors is handled privately; there is no public offering of the shares. In general, the shares of these businesses are less liquid, and their valuations are more difficult to determine.

An overwhelming majority of companies in the United States start as privately held companies. Private companies range in size and scope, encompassing the millions of closely held businesses in the U.S. The origin of a private company may be a family business that has grown well; the family may want to give it existence separate from the family, so they form a private company. For example, S.C. Johnson is a private company originally founded by Samuel Johnson; the family's fifth generation is currently leading the company. With revenue in excess of $10 billion and 13,000 employees worldwide, it is better organized as a private company rather than a family business. Because it is private, it still has the imprint of the family, which is even further reinforced by the presence of a family member at the helm.

Owners of a startup may decide to incorporate the business as a private company. Its success going forward depends on the leader's vision, dedication, and perseverance. While not all private companies thrive, there are instances of very large companies with decades-long tenure. Take, for example, Peter Kiewit Sons', Inc., Cargill, and Koch Industries. An engineering, mining, and construction company, Peter

Kiewit is an employee-owned private company started by two brothers in 1884; it is now a global company with 2017 revenues of $8.7 billion. Cargill and Koch Industries are much larger, with annual revenues in excess of $100 billion.

In terms of market capitalization among non-public companies, private companies lead the way; family businesses and non-profits in the U.S.A. contribute relatively less to the overall wealth in the economy. Investors in private companies include founders of the business, initial cadre of people who give shape to the founder's vision, angel investors, hedge funds, friends, and families. The number of shareholders is not large and no trading is permitted, except within the circle of investors. The separation of investors from management is not likely and perhaps not even desirable, for those who have the vision are also the investors. Such companies form the bedrock of innovation and growth in the economy; consequently, one barometer of a healthy economy is the growth in non-public companies. Since investors are involved in the management, and the company could borrow money from external entities, regulatory requirements are specified for the private companies, although these are unlikely to be as onerous as in a public company.

Private equity firms typically buy non-public companies at various stages in their lifecycle, make them profitable, and sell them to, or launch them as, public companies. Only seasoned investors with willingness to take a large stake in the business for a long term get involved in private equity investments. But this may change, for the SEC is considering opening up this avenue for investment for the masses. Even if this happens, investing in private equity may not fit the individual investor's goals and risk appetite. Even though returns could be high, there may be a wide range of returns among private equity firms, the investment may be tied up for the long term, and the outside investor's voice in the governance of the firm may be limited.

Formation

A privately held business can be formed in various ways: sole proprietorship, partnership, limited liability company, S-corporation, or C-corporation. A sole proprietorship is owned by a single owner; its legal status is not separate from the owner. All of the liabilities, assets, and owner equity of business belong to the proprietor who bears the risk of owning and running the business. The benefit to the owner is in terms of complete control and discretion over decisions related to the business. In a partnership, multiple owners share in the risks and returns of the entity; shared ownership spreads the risk across owners, some of whom may be active in the operation of the business. In limited liability companies (LLCs), many owners share in the risks and returns of the company. Such organizations have the benefit of limited liability of the owners without having to incorporate the entity. Sole proprietorship, partnership, and LLC are not classified as private companies.

Both S-corporations and C-corporations are incorporated under state laws. The distinction between the two is for tax purposes, which becomes apparent when a corporation approaches the IRS for registration as S-corporation or C-corporation. S-corporations are corporations that elect to pass corporate income, losses, deductions and credits to their shareholders for federal tax purposes. Pass throughs are reported by the individual shareholder when filing a tax return. An S-corporation must be a domestic corporation with only allowable shareholders (individuals, certain trusts, and estates) but not partnerships, corporations, or non-resident alien shareholders. S-corporations can have only one class of stock and can have no more than 100 shareholders. Certain types of businesses (e.g., financial institutions, insurance companies) are ineligible for incorporation as S-corporation.

The usual constrains placed upon S-corporations do not exist in the case of C-corporations. Limited shareholder liability, an unlimited number of shareholders, no restrictions on who can become a shareholder, choice of having more than one class of shares – these are all characteristics of a C-corporation, which can choose to be a private company or public company. If the corporation wants access to capital through financial markets, it needs to be organized as a C-corporation. Companies with one class of shares and no possibility of trading in the open market can choose to be S-corporations.

The formation of a private company begins with the incorporation of the company in a state. Although rules vary by state, major steps are somewhat comparable. The initiation requires a unique name, articles of incorporation, bylaws, etc. – much like in case of the launch of a public company.

Structure and Control

Most private companies are run by the founders or their representatives. Because of their hands-on approach, it is likely that, compared to a public company, the structure is somewhat fluid and control is not systemic or elaborate. As the business grows, owners would want a greater degree of control in order to manage the business risk. Even when governance measures are not obligatory, a growing business would likely benefit from voluntary steps toward systematic governance of the company. The organization structure should be formalized, with accountabilities assigned to each role, avoiding any overlaps and conflicts. A code of conduct should be adopted, internal controls over financial reporting (ICFR) should be instituted and calibrated as the business expands into newer ventures or global undertakings. ICFRs should be tested periodically and an independent audit of financial statements should be considered, even if not mandatory. While the immediate benefits of such measures may be vague, the company continues to shape its character through such endeavors. At the time of next big step, such as the IPO or a takeover by another company, it would be easier to prove what the company stands for.

Governance Challenges

Two related factors play a part in adding to the governance challenges of private companies. First, not all owners are separate from management and this causes a conflict of interest and fuzziness in fiduciary responsibility. Second, for the most part, private company governance measures are discretionary and therefore, the board and management may pay less attention to systemic governance measures. The mindset of minimizing the cost of governance may prevail, while the benefits are overlooked or bypassed.

In a private company, while there may be exceptions, the board is usually overrepresented by controlling shareholders and investors who may otherwise not be able to play the role of an independent director in monitoring and steering the corporation. A significant presence of interested investors on the board could result in silencing the other presumably independent voices on the board. Related party transactions may not all be in the interests of the company as conflicts of interest and influence prevails over decisions to hand out contracts and enter into transactions. Compromise of board credibility, integrity, and independence is likely in such cases.

Where the boards are strong, largely independent, and effective, they could enhance risk management oversight in a private company. The board can also extend its value by focusing on the company strategy, assessing the potential impact of innovation and emerging competition, approving company strategy, and improving merger and acquisition outcomes. Another area that can be improved by the board is succession planning. This is where in a private company, a degree of structure and discipline to evaluate the situation using data-driven discussion may be missing.

For a successful private company, one of the choices is to go public. Under its status as a private company, it may not have had the same discipline and rigor in its code of conduct as would be expected from a public company. For example, prospective investors would look carefully at related party transactions of the company to assess the nature and degree of conflict of interest by directors and senior management. To navigate through the transition from private to public, it is essential for the board to guide the company in improving governance sophistication, rigor, and effectiveness.

Finally, private companies are likely to benefit from greater attention to the financial accounting and reporting function. The ICFR may be optional for private companies, but the value of having strong controls over financial accounting and reporting cannot be overemphasized, even in a private company. Having qualified, competent personnel in this area is important, and their retention over time is equally critical. Without ample resources and adequate staff, the crucial role of the finance function cannot be accomplished. Inaccurate or incomplete financial information could mislead management and owners and could jeopardize the financial health of the company.

NON-PROFIT ORGANIZATIONS

Another relatively large number of non-public entities consists of not-for -profit (also called non-profit) organizations. Non-profits are incorporated in a state and have their separate legal personhood. Most non-profits work with limited resources, but they do perform an important role in the life of the society at large, and therefore need to be recognized and supported by appropriate laws and regulations.

Formation

A non-profit is incorporated under the laws of the state where it chooses to locate. Incorporators of a non-profit file information required for incorporation, most of which is included in the articles of incorporation of the entity. Once registered with the registrar of companies for the state, the organization can request for exemption from taxation under the federal and state laws. For obtaining tax exempt status, the entity should declare the purpose of the organization, which should not include the specific activities prohibited by the IRS for tax exempt filers. And although exempt, non-profits still have to file annual returns with tax authorities.

Structure and Control

With limited resources and lack of dedicated personnel, structure of non-profits remains vague and often undocumented. The non-profits typically have an executive director or equivalent position that is responsible for operations of the organization. The board of trustees (or directors) governs the entity while the executive director, along with the executive committee functions more like the management in a public company. The board is elected by members of the non-profit organization as defined in the articles of incorporation. With the exception of very few fulltime personnel, everyone else is a volunteer working to support the mission of the organization.

Control over the non-profit can vary across a wide spectrum, ranging from very loose to rather rigorous oversight. Generally, the greater the resources that the non-profit has, the stronger the watch over its actions. If monetary and in-kind contributions come from sources other than members, the donors would also exert some degree of influence in the governance process. A key concern of donors is if the entity is using their contributions according to the wishes expressed by them. Donors would also advocate that the organization uses its resources efficiently and gears spending toward achieving the set goals. To donors, the reliability of the governance process generates trust and confidence in the affairs of the non-profit.

Governance Challenges

A primary source of governance challenges is the volunteer workforce. Although they may have the mission of the organization at heart, they may not be informed or skilled for leading or managing the non-profit. Board members may have inadequate awareness of the governance process; they are willing to invest their time, but may not know what steps to take to manage risks of the entity. Add to this the problem of not having enough resources to garner expert help from outside, and the challenge becomes even more overwhelming.

In all volunteer organizations, the formation of a board slate is often organic. Those who have served for some time are likely to be recognized for a board seat. So, the protection of interests of the institution may not be in question. However, collectively, the body may not be as informed and skilled to drive the institution's mission. The nominating committee that puts forth the board slate should consciously work toward balancing the competency of the board. In this regard, it may be appropriate for the committee to seek people with specific knowhow to stand for the board election.

While striving to achieve the organization's mission, the board should ensure that its conduct is respected by those patrons whom the entity serves, donors who make contributions to the entity, and the society in which it is located. While the central focus of a public company is on the most recognized stakeholder – the shareholder – non-profits are naturally geared to multiple stakeholders, including beneficiaries, donors, and the society. Balancing the interests of multiple stakeholders can be a formidable task.

Non-profits are not exempt from challenges. The most recent challenge they face is ransomware, wherein the computer network is rendered inaccessible to the institution. If ransom is not paid within set time limit, the hackers threaten to erase files from the institution's database. Most non-profits have computer-based systems that run on volunteer time and a shoestring budget; as a result, these systems are vulnerable to hacks. The board must take adequate, cost effective steps to mitigate ransomware risks.

Additionally, many institutions are at risk of intrusion and killing by criminals who invade premises of non-profits – like churches, schools, hospitals – without much resistance. It is important for the boards to review the exposure, determine risk, and identify and implement cost effective procedures to mitigate the risk.

Finally, a non-profit board can certainly take the initiative to adopt governance measures that make sense for the institution they serve, especially if such steps are cost effective and would mitigate relevant risks. For example, the board could easily deliberate on and approve a code of conduct which will have a lasting impact on the institution and its stakeholders.

BIBLIOGRAPHY

Constable, S. 2019. Private equity looks to go downscale. *The Wall Street Journal* November 4, R6.

Davis, J. 2001. Governing the family-run business. Harvard Business School Working Knowledge, https://hbswk.hbs.edu/item/governing-the-family-run-business, Accessed September 2, 2019.

Krishnan, G. and Peytcheva, M. 2019. The risk of fraud in family firms: Assessment of external auditors. *Journal of Business Ethics* 157: 261–278.

Melilli, S. and Hughes, B. 2015. Private company governance: The call for sharper focus. *Forbes Insights*, in association with KPMG.

CHAPTER 15

Horizons of Corporate Governance

The field of corporate governance is constantly evolving. At the same time, the rate of advancement in the discipline has been impressive. As financial markets become more sophisticated, much larger in size, and more global in reach, the goal of protecting investor interests would gain even more traction. While a great deal has been done, there is much more to come.

Whereas the laws and regulations have taken the lead in defining threshold requirements of company governance, this alone is not enough. Indeed, if it were, there would be no more misbehaviors on the part of management, board, auditors, and other coregulators. The fact that financial frauds happen, restatements of financial statements occur, conflict of interest persists, and insider trading is prevalent suggests that there is room for improvement.

Broadly, root causes of many of the remaining problems appear to be human, that is, in the form of leadership and leader behavior, managerial motivation, group dynamics, and morality. This area is foreign to the laws and will have to be explored through rigorous empirical research rather than outright specification of rules. For now, the best that can be done is to find ways to notice anomalies in behavior and respond to the situation accordingly and perhaps without much support from the law. As experience accumulates and converges, there is a likelihood that best practices would emerge and eventually become principles or even requirements for effective governance.

In this chapter, a vast array of questions and topics are grouped under four topics: (1) business environment, (2) company lifecycle stage, structure, and size, (3) corporate governance ecosystem, and (4) regulation and compliance.

BUSINESS ENVIRONMENT

Undoubtedly, the world is "shrinking"; there is no place too far. The only formidable constraint is the political boundaries that could create fences like tariffs, operational constraints, taxes, and other laws. But even here, a country's interest lies in growth through globalization; inviting businesses to camp out in their backyard is an important tenet for most nations around the world.

Global competition means more pressure on management to understand the culture of the community where they want to do business, decipher the nature of local competition, comprehend laws of the land, and tread carefully on the political front. All of these are stress factors in addition to those encountered in domestic competition. Besides, the political-economic forces of the domiciled country could play a part. For example, technology that is sensitive in the nation's defense may not be shared with foreign countries. The U.S.A. has expressed concern, for example, with the way Huawei Technologies provides 5G products and services to its foreign customers; the fear is that some of the information it collects through its products and services may be shared with China's political machinery. While the picture would become clear in the future, Corporate America would be reluctant to cut deals with Huawei today. Companies with global presence have more governance challenges on hand than a company that operates only within the USA.

The diversity of governance systems and processes around the world was insightfully acknowledged by Sir Adrian Cadbury. As markets become borderless and the flow of financial resources into investments turns into a global phenomenon, free flow of information that is reliable and transparent is necessary to support investment decisions. While markets and investors may be facilitated by seamless connectivity across regions of the world, political boundaries could work as hurdles. As a result, fights over jurisdictions will continue to persist. China, for example, has its own perspective on how to shape corporate governance, and so does the European Union. Political powers can influence access to markets and information, and the reliability of such information.

A U.S. company's auditors, for example, may rely on auditors in China to conduct audits of operations there. If the auditors fail to deliver assurance of reliability of financial information, the shareholders would be at risk. To compound the matter further, Beijing does not allow U.S. authorities such as the PCAOB to inspect audits of Chinese companies listed on the American stock exchanges. Such matters need to be resolved to achieve the overall goal of access to reliable information almost anywhere the investor seeks opportunities.

The world is a mosaic of ideologies. Different regions have their own unique perspectives on globally-relevant issues and challenges. These include privacy, confidentiality, ethical conduct, and neutrality in access. The European Union, for example, has a very strong view on privacy rights, and has accordingly launched a new rule called General Data Protection Regulation (GDPR), which focuses on getting an assurance that users know, understand, and consent to the data collected about them. Search engine providers like Google have faced considerable scrutiny around the world in regards to the way they share data with users.

Looking forward, it does not appear that global diversity will dissolve into a single, uniform governance picture for the world. Corporations doing business worldwide will have to tolerate the diversity and comply with local and regional requirements. While this is an added burden, the potential for a company's growth probably outweighs the cost of being present in the region. This is precisely the draw in doing business in populous countries such as China and India.

Technology as a Disrupter

It is now well established that technology continues to disrupt the existing mode of doing business. Such disruption causes a redefinition of jobs, shift in business model, and even displacement of older competitors. The financial technology revolution, called fintech, has impacted payment card industry, banks, and other financial services firms. The plethora of payment options in today's nearly cashless society is staggering in both numbers and creativity, and plastic cards seem to give way to other options. Smartphones have taken on the role of a pervasive transaction device, anywhere from boarding a flight to paying for Coke.

An important development, often struggling along the way, is in the field of cyber currency. Because of lack of a traditional financial system as a backup to its operations, which normally would lead to trust in the system, the cybercurrency experiments have proven to be volatile. The most recent foray in the field .by Facebook seems to have an eye on a complete solution via an appropriate ecosystem and proper backing of funds to support the transaction system. However, Facebook is facing considerable doubt from currency regulators and the federal reserve bank. Meanwhile, the blockchain technology residing at the core of eCurrency has been found to be versatile; myriad applications of the blockchain technology are in progress and the development is truly promising.

Today's business transformations thrive on communications technology. As 5G networks become ubiquitous, more changes are expected. One area that is likely to grow is the Internet of Things (IoT). Of course, speed and rate of data transfer will impact practically everything for which the Internet is utilized, so the impact can be expected to be far-reaching.

Cloud computing was born out of the need to share expensive infrastructure and data storage solutions. A common need, but individually expensive solutions bring businesses to cloud services, a cost-effective option for small and large companies alike. The idea of sharing did not stop here; it grew into a whole new revolution often called Uberization. Using information technology, it changes the market for a service by helping flexible supply meet immediate demand for the service. Airbnb releases the untapped capacity of households with bedrooms to host guests overnight. Uber and Lyft operate driver-owned fleets of vehicles to provide ride for those who need it, almost anywhere, anytime. DoorDash, Uber Eats, GrubHub and Postmates are among the new crop of companies that specialize in restaurant delivery and take-out. In another initiative, people subscribing to MoviePass fill the cinema theaters, improving capacity utilization. WeWork, a subsidiary of We Company, offers flexible space and coworking facilities in many locations around the world, moving businesses to locations they can afford to use at any scale.

Those in charge of governance will have to ask: what would these and other disruptions mean to their company? How does the change impact their company's competitive strength, survivability, and profitability? And what can be done to manage the risk of losing to new competition? At times, there may not be any options for the company, except to embrace change and calibrate internal processes and controls to adapt to the change. Any strategic map drawn by management could get derailed within a short period of time due to technology shifts; it is the duty of management along with the board to keep their guard up and take timely strategic action, not only to neutralize impact of the disruption, but possibly find a strategic niche to exploit the change for the benefit of the company and its stakeholders.

Cybersecurity

Cyber attacks are pervasive, cutting across all walks of life and society. Such attacks are attempted remotely, sometimes from a place where the actor cannot be disciplined through legal action. Such anonymous criminal acts can result in loss of data, unavailability of systems and programs, and disruption of services. The latest version of cyber attacks is called ransomware, where the attacker asks for a price; only upon payment – usually in cyber currency to maintain anonymity – will the attacker decrypt data on the victim's system.

Sure enough, the SEC has noticed cybersecurity risks to which companies are exposed. The Division of Corporate Finance of the U.S. Securities and Exchange Commission issued in 2011 guidance expressing the Division's views on disclosure obligations relating to cybersecurity risks and cyber incidents. That guidance, which is neither a rule, regulation or statement of the SEC, was intended to assist registrants in assessing what, if any, disclosures should be provided about cybersecurity matters in light of each registrant's specific facts and circumstances. Many publicly traded companies added new cybersecurity risk disclosures following this guidance. This change in reporting practices provides investors with an opportunity to assess the impact of new cybersecurity disclosures.

Directors must understand cybersecurity as a management issue. Technology enables today's cybersecurity attacks; however, these need to be addressed in a holistic manner as conscious, risk-based decisions. At a minimum, they should understand the legal implications of cyber risks to the company, how to mitigate such risks, and how to provide a response in the event of an attack. Conceivably, the board can't be an expert on every issue. If cyber security or any other challenges warrant bringing on board appropriate consultants, the board should not hesitate to do so. Any cybersecurity solutions implemented by management must be nested in the overall enterprise-wide risk management framework adopted by the company.

Cybersecurity is just one example of heightened risk exposures due to the Internet. There are other technology-based risks, such as the third-party risks sourced in a party (e.g., supplier) linked to the company's systems. Global value-chain implemented by many businesses these days warrants that risks emanating from third parties should be carefully identified and mitigated.

COMPANY LIFECYCLE STAGE, STRUCTURE, AND SIZE

The more advanced the company in its lifecycle, the greater the likelihood of its stability and reliability. A 100-year-old company presumably can manage risks better than a ten-year-old company, although there are no absolute guarantees. An incubation or initiation stage company can be subject to infant mortality; a contagion stage company is simply focused on growth and may disregard other crucial signals such as cutting corners on ethical front. A mature company is more like a steady ship; it likely is experienced in identifying and managing risks to the benefit of its stakeholders.

With growth comes a larger complement of employees, diverse suppliers, and many different customers. This occurs not just locally but worldwide. Growth increases the size, but more importantly, it adds to the complexity of how the business is conducted. A business structure ideal for a small company may not be appropriate for a fast-growing enterprise. Identifying responsibilities, aligning accountability with change, and monitoring all aspects of value chain present challenges for a growing company. Often, growth is accompanied by the need to invest more in the business, resulting in a cash crunch.

Financing such growth and ensuring that it will materialize in positive earnings over time is an important obligation of a growing company's management and the board.

Does Size Matter?

SEC has exempted small public companies from certain regulatory requirements. In 2019, the SEC considered a proposal to exempt more small companies from certain audit requirements. The idea is to lighten the regulatory burden so that the business that is supposedly struggling to survive and grow will have money to drive profits. The rationale behind this decision seems to be that smaller firms may find these requirements overly burdensome and arguably without harnessing intended benefits.

A position supporting favorable treatment of newer, smaller companies may presumably attract some benefits. For example, it is likely this may be seen as an incentive to new companies. As a result, incorporation of public companies in the formative stage may increase, and this may lead to economic growth. For example, bypassing financial audits in the early stages of a company seems financially beneficial, for it will save money. However, the shareholders may wonder if the financial statements are reliable. Early stages of formation and growth are the ones where slippage in reliable financial reporting could occur intentionally or otherwise. Errors and omissions in financial reporting could result in later restatements, but these would not protect investors from damage done to their investment value. The formation stage is the window of time in a company's life where the implementation of a control framework would likely produce lasting benefits in risk management. The argument of financial reprieve disregards the fact that a public company has access to capital markets and therefore, is obligated to be truthful, transparent, and timely in its engagement with investors. So, the regulatory burden as an isolated view without regard to fiduciary obligations is hollow. Perhaps in some regulatory matters the pressure to grant such concessions may be purely political and cannot be easily defeated.

Practically, a perspective on small versus large is relative, requiring a heuristic understanding of where one wants to draw the line. This boundary may be shifting over time, and at any given time, there may be more than one such line drawn, applicable to different contexts.

Comparing companies with various accommodations in governance requirements would be a challenge for the investor. Ultimately, what is good for one company applies to others as well, and exceptions based on size, however measured, may just be conceptually indefensible.

Intuitively, it appears that small businesses may transgress into wrongdoing if they are not required to grow in a disciplined manner. In this regard, some of the regulations that may appear burdensome may in fact be most needed for the young, growing companies. For example, the adoption of a code of conduct in early stages would allow the firm to grow with a clear understanding of the nature of organization and its policies. Larger, more seasoned corporations have presumably gone through the exercise in their early stages, so the ongoing benefit to them from the code of conduct is relatively automatic. If a small firm is exempt from having to adopt its own code of conduct, it simply may be counterproductive.

Are Startups Different?

Startups by definition appear to be small. In the technology space, startups perceived as promising are chased by investors in the hunt for superior returns. When the glut of funding makes the bargain attractive for the startup, the tendency is to accept the investment. Having relieved itself from a major worry (where would the capital come from?), the innovators adopt a single focus of honing their innovation with a view to head out to the market as soon as possible. In the process, both the innovators and the investors may have overlooked the moral fabric of the organization.

Could this argument sustain when a startup has been around for some years and has attracted considerable additional equity? Perhaps. There is no guarantee that a whole lot of effort will be exerted by the entrepreneurs in giving a moral identity to the company; if anything, the desire to seek material goals becomes more dominant because the business is now adequately financed. The case of We Company included in Table 15.1 illustrates the point.

CORPORATE GOVERNANCE ECOSYSTEM

Because the shareholder is at the core of governance goals, it is important to recognize questions related to company ownership.

TABLE 15.1 We Company – filing for initial public offering (IPO)

In 2019, We Company, the flexible space, coworking startup filed with the SEC for IPO. Through its subsidiaries the company buys, leases, or rents properties and converts such real estate into flexible space that is ideal for small companies that do not wish to or cannot afford to own or rent large space for business. We Company has grown greatly since its launch, establishing its footprint in several countries, although it has not yet turned profitable.

In the early stages of business development, what a firm does as a private company may be wholly focused on business growth and financing. In the process, governance takes a second seat; those who contribute to the business and financing of the business become closely attached to the company as investors in the future of the startup. For example, four of the seven non-employee directors are representatives of stockholders, such as the Softbank, and one of the directors is in the real estate business, acquiring properties suitable for flexible space rental business. Only one director appears to have no financing or business ties with the company. The question is: can those who represent major investors effectively represent *all* shareholders of a public company?

So, the close ties and conflicts of interest require unwinding. For example, Adam Neumann owns the majority of supervoting shares with 20 votes per share, thus leaving control of the company at his discretion. He has borrowed funds from the company to buy shares in the company. His wife, Rebekah Neumann, is deeply involved in the business development, although she does not take any salary. Other relatives of the Naumann family also take part in occasional real estate deals of the company. The web of related parties and related party transactions is embedded in the company's business.

While related party transactions are not illegal, it is expected that such transactions would work in the company's interests, not the other party. Contractual relationships with related parties could result in diverting company resources, well beyond the benefits received, to others in the inner circle of the founders.

It appears the board has only two independent directors, both of whom will serve on the audit committee. As a company that is controlled by majority voting rights of its founder, Adam Neumann, the company in its filing says that it hopes to be exempt from the requirement that the compensation committee and the nominating and corporate governance committee should comprise of independent directors. Finally, the founder occupies both board chair and chief executive positions.

The message is simple. Private companies have considerable flexibility in how they obtain equity or how they run business. When going public, some of these ways of doing business may run short on transparency and disclosure. An egregious outlay of company resources also may result from the practices set by a private company before going public. Management should be prepared, both in mind and action, to bear the fiduciary

(Continued)

TABLE 15.1 (Cont.)

responsibility to all shareholders, for it would be a public company. And founders should strive to get away from thinking that the company is their "baby" and they are entitled to conduct business any way they like. Access to investors at large comes with responsibilities, and businesses issuing a call for IPO must first get ready to demonstrate that they are prepared for the fiscal discipline. Perhaps We Company will emerge as a good example of governance once it sorts out some of these challenges of shifting from a private to a public domain.

A director conscientiously working on behalf of the shareholders has to visualize whose interests the director is representing sitting in the boardroom. Increasingly, individual investors are outpaced by institutional investors; thus, the focus shifts to knowing institutional investors with stakes in the company. The problem of focusing on the shareholder, even among the institutional investors, could become more aggravated as the choices of investment vehicles – Mutual Funds and ETFs – shrink to a few very large, dominant, and powerful channels of investment. In the future, only a handful of investment vehicles may be involved in making up the entire body of outstanding shares.

Perhaps this diffusion of identification of the persona of shareholder could be a boon to the current momentum toward accountability toward not just shareholders, but the entire stakeholder group. Private equity firms have no problem in identifying their investors; they are less likely to be asked about other stakeholders, except in the context of compliance with legal and regulatory requirements. For public companies, the future lies in balancing the interests of other stakeholders versus those of the shareholder. Without nurturing other stakeholders, the interests of shareholders may not be delivered as well.

Sustainability

The emphasis on maximization of shareholder returns in the long run is unlikely to be displaced; however, it will be increasingly shaped by concerns for other stakeholders, including the community at large, the nation, and the world. Issues of sustainability, both of an entity and the environment in which it thrives, are now at the front and center of the governance challenge. Climate change, alternative energy sources, green living, etc. will become germane to almost every organization. You can't do good to your investors unless you take care of the universe around the corporation. This challenge of optimizing across all stakeholders will tax both management and the board in the future. Experiments of the idea of a triple-bottom line which includes corporate social responsibility (CSR), have been in play for some time and will continue to gain ground as a potentially viable metric.

The Board

The search for board members who are capable, available, interested, and independent will continue to become even more intense. As a group, diversity of the board will be under the microscope of investors. One very influential fund announced recently that it will be looking for at least two women on the board of companies targeted for investment. This illustrates a larger point, namely that the voice of large investors and institutional investors will continue to gain strength and will not easily be disregarded.

Multiple directorships of board members will also come under scrutiny, for it represents a double-edged sword. Well-connected board members could help the company benefit from their relationship; however, representation on multiple boards splits time and attention at a time when governance becomes a critical matter for the company, its shareholders, and the regulators.

REGULATION AND COMPLIANCE

The SOX and Dodd-Frank Act introduced significant sophistication in the field of governance, mostly in the spirit of problems caused by bad behavior on the part of corporations or industries. Independence of regulators is further emphasized and a clear link is established between the independent auditors and the audit committee of the board. Additionally, management's responsibility for truthfulness of the financial information is clarified. Such measures help in improving governance.

Balance between the Market and Statutory Regulation

Regulation is a tightrope exercise in balancing political, economic, and business interests. The role of regulation is to require entities to perform particular actions while prohibiting others. The overarching idea is to bring the behavior of governed and those in charge of governance to an acceptable level. Overall, the intentions are reasonable from the viewpoint that if the government does not protect, who else could do so? Enforcement of regulation is a punitive measure that attempts to bring some balance in the economic behavior of organizations and their managers.

Unfortunately, as new regulations grow without limits, there is no real justification needed to bring on yet another regulation. But regulators are rarely incentivized to propose removal of any rules in place. The situation is comparable to what happens with curriculum at universities. The faculty and administrators expand their curricular programs by adding courses, diplomas, and degrees. However, there rarely is a proposal to cut any of the courses, no matter how dated, from the catalog. Universities may put forth an argument that "dead" curricula do not impose any harm to anyone, so why worry? In contrast, once in place, regulations have the force of law and continue to remain a burden on the economy. In some cases, this may be true even when the goal behind such regulation is gone or worthless. Unless there is a trigger that would require action to cut regulation, not much happens in bureaucracies and clans. Some states in the USA have adopted a zero-base budget: all rules come to a halt unless they are explicitly triggered back in time. Such a move often is accompanied by a dictate on the ratio of rules activated to the total number of existing rules (e.g., 1:2, one rule initiated for every two subject to sunset).

There is a cost to compliance with regulations. A Mercatus Center Study on cumulative cost of regulations estimates that in the year 2012, the average annual cost of compliance added up to $4 trillion – a 0.8% growth reduction of the economy – because of two main sources:

- Regulatory interventions affect investment choices, with cumulative costs well past the cost of compliance.

- The accumulation of regulation over time results in progressively greater disfigurement because knowledge creation slows or is absent, which suffocates economic push.

Is this regulatory burden uneven across different size companies? Does the size matter when making a decision if small companies should be exempt from a particular regulation? Is the lifecycle stage of a company important in deliberating such decisions? Or, could we assume that lifecycle stage is implicit in the company size?

To address overregulation, a holistic approach is necessary. Executive orders may not be enough to rebalance the weight of regulations on all aspects of the economy, including corporate governance. Systemic changes through passage of legislation are required. Recently witnessed slowing of the growth in regulations is a welcome sign, but a systematic reduction in accumulated regulations is a pressing need.

Finally, it is important that each regulation bears some connection to research. Ignoring research while adding new regulations or reviewing the existing ones is counterproductive, for good research shows what works and what does not. To quote Sir Adrian Cadbury, "we call to halt codes, laws and regulations in this field to give time for theory to catch up with practical experience and illuminate it."

Perhaps a lot has passed through the legislative process in the past without a conscious examination of its usefulness, maybe because no relevant research was found to corroborate the requirement. In any case, to keep the trust of those required to comply, it is important for the regulators to test their requirements against available studies and relevant conceptual models.

The sheer volume of regulations is one thing; the effectiveness of each regulation is another. Often reacting – perhaps overreacting – to an economic catastrophe, lawmakers lean on overprescribing. Before they are mandated, do regulations go through a litmus test of cost effectiveness? This is another path of inquiry that may lead to the identification of unnecessary regulatory burden.

FUTURE ISSUES AND CHALLENGES

Corporate governance has been around for centuries, although the degree of sophistication infused in it is relatively recent. One might wonder why so many surprises emerge almost regularly; after all, the field of corporate governance is not new. The core of corporate governance rests in human behavior, and it is not easy to modify or regulate management, board, or auditor behavior. Here are some examples:

- Conflict of interest can appear quickly, without conscious awareness of, or control over, it. People are weak in identifying such conflicts, and when identified, dealing with them properly. The Baltimore, Maryland, mayor had to quit her prestigious post of mayor because her book was purchased in volumes by those interested in pleasing her.

- It is easy to blame pressure in doing wrong things. However, pressure is often internal and the individual experiencing such pressure must endure it. To blame pressure is inappropriate; it is not an escape valve for any compromises.

- Maturity, or motivation, to deal with the issue may be lacking. Newer board members, for example, are more vulnerable because they are not experienced in looking at situations in larger context.

- Rewards and relationships might be too attractive to strike a challenge to something that is "fishy." In one experiment reported by Dan Ariely, judges of artwork who were compensated regardless of how they rated artwork were biased in favor of the institution that paid their fees. The fees were not tied to the decision, but the judges still rewarded those who paid their fees.

- Courage is a very personal thing.

- The law is always way behind the times. Regulatory measures could be ineffective, especially when they fail to guide behavior. In the Boeing 737 MAX disasters under investigation, it became apparent that the regulators at the FAA relied too much on the company engineers in approving the jet as safe for flying. Private ordering of one's regulatory duty makes ineffective the very step that is supposed to guarantee risk mitigation. The situation is much like company audits by independent auditors, where the reliance placed on the evidence submitted by the auditee could result in poor audit quality and perhaps faulty financial information.

- Power corrupts. Influential managers could use their influence in many ways to pull off a wrongdoing.

- Disposition rules. As discussed in Chapter 13, disposition of the executive could make him vulnerable to moral temptation, which could lead to fraud. Self-regarding and narcissistic leaders could easily get blindsided in doing their moral duty, although they are otherwise excellent performers.

As the above list illustrates, it is the human that stands at the core of not doing the right thing. While changes on many fronts help improve the governance outlook, not being able to address the human side fully and properly is a major void. For the foreseeable time, this is not likely to change, even though research is underway to examine the core issue of human behavior as it relates to corporate governance. Meanwhile, directors, auditors, and other coregulators will have to be vigilant in scanning the environment for potential irregularities emanating from the human psyche. And that is a laudable task!

BIBLIOGRAPHY

Cadbury, A. 1992. *A Report of the Committee on the Financial Aspects of Corporate Governance (The Cadbury Report)*. London: Gee and Co. Ltd.

Coffey, B., McLaughlin, P. A. and Peretto, P. 2016. *The Cumulative Cost of Regulations*. Mercatus Working Paper, Mercatus Center, George Mason University.

Cyber-Risk Oversight Executive Summary, Handbook Series 2014 Edition. National Association of Corporate Directors (NACD) in collaboration with AIG and Internet Security Alliance (ISA), Washington, DC.

Morse, E. A., Raval, V. and Wingender, J. R., Jr. 2017. SEC cybersecurity guidelines: Insights into the utility of risk factor disclosures for investors. *The Business Lawyer*, Winter 2017–2018.

Rai, S. 2014. *Cybersecurity: What the Board of Directors Need to Ask*. Altamonte Springs, FL: Institute of Internal Auditors Research Foundation.

The We Company. 2019. Form S-1 (as filed with the SEC on August 14). www.sec.gov/Archives/edgar/data/1533523/000119312519220499/d781982ds1.htm#toc781982_102, Accessed September 10, 2019.

List of Acronyms

AC	Audit Committee of the board of directors
ACFE	Audit Committee Financial Expert
ACG	Aspirational Corporate Governance
ADR	American Depository Receipt
AGM	Annual General Meeting
AICPA	American Institute of Certified Public Accountants
BSC	The Balanced Scorecard
CAE	Chief Audit Executive
CAM	Critical Audit Matter
CEO	Chief Executive Officer
CFO	Chief Financial Officer
CIA	Certified Internal Auditor
CISA	Certified Information Systems Auditor
CISO	Chief Information Security Officer
COBIT	Control OBjectives for Information and related Technologies
COSO	Committee Of Sponsoring Organizations of the Treadway Commission
CPA	Certified Public Accountant
CSA	Control Self-Assessment
CSR	Corporate Social Responsibility
CUPC	California Public Utilities Commission
DFM	Disposition-based Fraud Model
EBITDA	Earnings Before Interest, Taxes, Depreciation, and Amortization
ERP	Enterprise Resource Planning
ETF	Exchange-Traded Fund

FASB	Financial Accounting Standards Board
FCC	Federal Communications Commission
FDA	Food and Drug Administration
GAAP	Generally Accepted Accounting Principles
GDPR	General Data Protection Regulation
GRC	Governance, Risk, and Compliance
IAF	Internal Audit Function
IASB	International Accounting Standards Board
ICFR	Internal Controls over Financial Reporting
IIA	Institute of Internal Auditors
IPO	Initial Public Offering
IoT	Internet of Things
IRS	Internal Revenue Service
MD&A	Management Discussion & Analysis
NACD	National Association of Corporate Directors
NASDAQ	National Association of Securities Dealers Automated Quotations
NEO	Named Executive Officer
OECD	Organization for Economic Cooperation and Development
PCAOB	Public Company Accounting Oversight Board
RSU	Restricted Stock Unit
SEC	Securities and Exchange Commission
SOP	Say on Pay
SOX	The Sarbanes-Oxley Act
TCT	Transaction Cost Theory
TPRM	Third Party Risk Management
XBRL	eXtensible Business Reporting Language

List of Web-Based Resources

aicpa.org (American Institute of Certified Public Accountants)
auditanalytics.com
boardsource.org
businessroundtable.org
conference-board.org
corpgov.law.harvard.edu (Harvard Law School Forum on Corporate Governance and Financial Regulation)
corporatecomplianceinsights.com
deloitte.com/us/en/pages/center-for-board-effectiveness
ey.com/en_us/board-matters
fasb.org (Financial Accounting Standards Board)
fcdoc.org (Forum for corporate directors)
globalcorporategovernance.com
greatboards.org
investopedia.com
home.kpmg/ie/en/home/services/audit/audit-committee-institute.html
millstein.law.columbia.edu (Ira M. Millstein Center for Global Markets and Corporate Ownership)
na.theiia.org (Institute of Internal Auditors)
nacd.org
pcaobus.org (Public Company Accounting Oversight Board)
pwc.com/us/en/services/governance-insights-center.html
sec.gov
societycorpgov.org
thenonprofittimes.com
weinberg.udel.edu (John L. Weinberg Center for Corporate Governance)

Index

Page numbers in **bold** font refer to content in **figures;** page numbers in *italics* refer to content in *tables.*

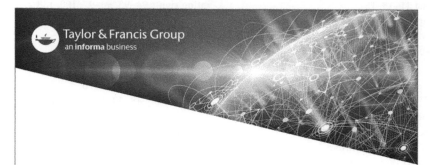

Milton Keynes UK
Ingram Content Group UK Ltd.
UKHW031532071024
449327UK00005B/105

9 780367 468866